Early praise for *Programming Ecto*

Let's face it, Ecto is not a small library. I think Darin and Eric did a fantastic job of breaking it all down into understandable pieces, giving a ton of examples along the way. You'll learn how to use Ecto, and perhaps more importantly, how it was meant to be used. And if you think you know it very well already, I'm sure you'll learn new things too!

➤ **Wojtek Mach**
 Hex Core Team, Consultant at Plataformatec

It does a great job of not only explaining how to use Ecto, but also illuminating the SQL underneath and the design decisions that the Ecto team made when building it. For a new team, this would be a great book to teach with; likewise, for an experienced team, this makes for a good reference book.

➤ **Ben Marx**
 Software Architect, Bleacher Report

This is a useful guide for beginners, but also a great resource for developers that have a medium level of knowledge of Ecto. I learned new tricks reading this book.

➤ **Ulisses De Almeida**
 Elixir Developer, author of *Learn Functional Programming with Elixir*

For many Elixir projects, Ecto is your most important partner, so it's important to learn to use it effectively. Darin and Eric have created a wonderful roadmap to help beginners and experienced developers explore its powerful feature set. It's full of clear examples that will help you quickly master Ecto—finish this book and you'll be well on your way to creating powerful, scalable, reliable, and maintainable database applications.

➤ **Bryan Stearns**
   Senior Software Engineer and Consultant

An eloquent discussion of the tools Ecto provides for database programming in Elixir: testing with sandboxes, changesets, embedded schemas, polymorphic associations, and much more. This book will be a reference for most engineers working in Elixir and Ecto.

➤ **Matt Milton**
   Software Engineer, Enbala Power Networks

Programming Ecto

Build Database Apps in Elixir for Scalability and Performance

Darin Wilson
Eric Meadows-Jönsson

The Pragmatic Bookshelf

Raleigh, North Carolina

Many of the designations used by manufacturers and sellers to distinguish their products are claimed as trademarks. Where those designations appear in this book, and The Pragmatic Programmers, LLC was aware of a trademark claim, the designations have been printed in initial capital letters or in all capitals. The Pragmatic Starter Kit, The Pragmatic Programmer, Pragmatic Programming, Pragmatic Bookshelf, PragProg and the linking *g* device are trademarks of The Pragmatic Programmers, LLC.

Every precaution was taken in the preparation of this book. However, the publisher assumes no responsibility for errors or omissions, or for damages that may result from the use of information (including program listings) contained herein.

Our Pragmatic books, screencasts, and audio books can help you and your team create better software and have more fun. Visit us at *https://pragprog.com*.

The team that produced this book includes:

Publisher: Andy Hunt
VP of Operations: Janet Furlow
Managing Editor: Susan Conant
Series Editor: Bruce A. Tate
Development Editor: Jacquelyn Carter
Copy Editor: Kim Cofer
Indexing: Potomac Indexing, LLC
Layout: Gilson Graphics

For sales, volume licensing, and support, please contact *support@pragprog.com*.

For international rights, please contact *rights@pragprog.com*.

ISBN-13: 978-1-68050-282-4
Book version: P1.0—April 2019

Contents

Acknowledgments

As the book's authors, we're the lucky ones who get to have our names on the front cover. But without the extra effort and support of many other folks, this book would have been a fraction of what it currently is, if it existed at all.

We're deeply grateful to Bruce Tate for originally suggesting the idea to us, and for sharing the wisdom gathered from the many books he's written over the years. Our editor Jackie Carter did an extraordinary job guiding a pair of nervous first-time authors with insight, editorial acumen, and a seemingly endless supply of patience. José Valim made himself available at several points in the process to clarify behavior we weren't sure of, and help us stay on top of features in upcoming releases.

We'd also like thank the reviewers who gave us much-needed feedback on the book as it was evolving: Olufemi Adeojo, Ulisses De Almeida, Mike Foster, Elias Karakoulakis, Justin Lane, Wojtek Mach, Ben Marx, Sean Miller, Matt Milton, Kim Shrier, and Stefan Turalski. And big thanks to the many beta readers who sent in errata to the Pragmatic Bookshelf website—this book would have a lot more errors if not for the efforts of these folks.

Darin Wilson

I'd like to send thanks and shout-outs to my teammates at Infinite Red, especially the leadership team (Jamon Holmgren, Ken Miller, and Todd Werth) for steering us toward Elixir in the first place. And extra gratitude is to due to my fellow Elixirists: Daniel Berkompas, Zach Berkompas, Ryan Linton, Yulian Glukhenko, Morgan Laco, and Silas Matson. Their pull requests and code reviews have taught me more about Elixir than they'll ever know.

Finally, I'd like to thank the loves of my life, my wife Jessica and daughter Ella. I'd need a book ten times this size to tell you how grateful I feel to have you both in my life. Thank you for all the love, inspiration, support, and laughter.

Eric Meadows-Jönsson

I'd like to thank José Valim, first of course for creating Elixir but primarily for mentoring me through the initial development of Ecto. When Ecto was created I was still new to Elixir as almost everyone was back then, before the release of Elixir 1.0. José helped guide me through the process of creating Ecto and taught me about Elixir and OSS development. José eventually invited me to be a core part of the development of Elixir itself which I am very grateful for.

I would also like to thank Bruce Tate, the series editor of this book. Bruce hired me right out of school when Elixir was still in its infancy and made a bet on Elixir and on me, which allowed me to continue to work with Elixir.

Introduction

For as long as there have been databases, there have been programmers writing libraries to access those databases in a more friendly way.

Which is a nice way of saying that they've been trying to avoid writing SQL.

SQL is powerful—there's a reason it's stuck around as long as it has—but generating it manually is tedious and error-prone. Developers have addressed this problem by creating libraries that wrap up the low-level vagaries of talking to a database into an API that's more harmonious with the language being used. In Java, we had Hibernate. In Python, SQLAlchemy. In Ruby, ActiveRecord and DataMapper. And now in Elixir, we have Ecto.

Ecto is a large library, and even with its excellent documentation, it can be hard to know where to start. This book will help you with that. Just as it's helpful to have a tour guide when visiting a new city, this book will help you find your way through Ecto. We'll take you through what we believe is the optimal path for learning the major components, and along the way you'll get expert advice and insight from one of Ecto's creators. At the end, you'll have a solid working knowledge of Ecto and you'll be ready to start integrating it into your own projects.

Who This Book Is For

This book is for developers who want to access relational databases from their Elixir applications. This includes applications that use the Phoenix web development framework, but Ecto can work in any Elixir app, whether it uses Phoenix or not.

We're going to assume you have some basic knowledge of Elixir. You should be comfortable with creating and running Elixir applications, as well as the basic components of the language: modules, functions, pattern matching, working with the pipe operator, and so on. If you're brand new to the language, you might want to get some experience under your belt before diving into Ecto. *Programming Elixir ≥ 1.6 [Tho18]* is a great place to start.

We're also going to assume that you're comfortable working with relational databases and SQL. You don't need to be an expert, but you should be familiar with tables, columns, indexes, and how to write queries. Many online tutorials are available that can teach you the basics.

What's In This Book

The book is divided into two parts. The first part will walk you through the main modules that form the core of Ecto's functionality. The second part will build on that knowledge and apply it to real-world use cases that often come up with database programming.

Throughout both parts, you'll be practicing what you learn by working on a sample app that's included with the book. We'll talk more about that in Chapter 1, Getting Started with Repo, on page 3.

Part I - Ecto Fundamentals

Part I is a tour of Ecto's API. We'll start at the ground level with the most basic features that Ecto provides, then work our way up, module-by-module, through all of the core features of the library. You'll be writing code every step of the way to help get Ecto into your fingers. At the end of Part I, you'll have a solid understanding of the API, and experience using it in working code.

Part II - Ecto Applied

Part II will take the knowledge you picked up in Part I and put it to work. Each chapter covers a specific task or use case that you're likely to run into as you start integrating Ecto into your projects. You'll learn things like integrating Ecto with Phoenix, running tests asynchronously, working with custom types, streaming large datasets, and the like.

How To Read This Book

You should start by reading Part I in order, from start to finish. Part I covers the most important features of Ecto and each chapter builds on the one before. Even if you've done some work with Ecto before, it's best not to skip around too much, as you might miss out on some key features you weren't aware of.

Part II is much less strict. You can read the chapters in any order, and you should feel free to focus your attention on the topics that are most interesting to you, and leave the rest for another time.

Online Resources

You can download all the example source code for the book from the Pragmatic Bookshelf website for this book.[1] You can also provide feedback by submitting errata entries.

If you're reading the book in PDF form, you can click the link above a code listing to view or download the specific examples.

Ready to dive in? Open a terminal window and your favorite editor, and let's get started.

---

1. https://pragprog.com/book/wmecto/programming-ecto

Part I

Ecto Fundamentals

We begin by gradually learning the core features of Ecto's API. Each chapter in this part covers a different Ecto module, starting with the basics, then working toward more complex use cases. It's best to read this part in order from start to finish. You'll then have the foundation you need to look at the specific use cases covered in Part II.

## CHAPTER 1

Getting Started with Repo

Welcome to Ecto!

If you're one of the majority of users who needs to use Elixir with a database, you're in luck: Ecto is the most prominent persistence framework for Elixir. Actively developed since its introduction in 2014, Ecto is mature, stable, and well-supported by an enthusiastic community of developers that includes members of the Elixir core team.

Ecto is the default database library that ships with the Phoenix web development framework, so for many developers, working with Phoenix is their first introduction to Ecto. Ecto works well with Phoenix, but it's a completely separate project and you can use it in any Elixir app. In fact, aside from a couple of chapters in Part II, we won't be discussing Phoenix at all in this book. We'll stay focused on Ecto itself.

In this chapter, we'll start with the basics. We'll get a brief overview of Ecto as a whole, then set up a small sample app so that you can try out the code you're learning as we go. We'll then take a close look at the Repo module, which is the heart of Ecto and the springboard for the rest of this part of the book.

Ecto and Elixir

Ecto is not the only database library for Elixir, but it's one of the most mature and best-supported. Plataformatec, the company that launched Elixir, has been involved in Ecto's development since the beginning, and José Valim is still a frequent committer.

But beyond Ecto's pedigree, three main characteristics make it stand out.

First, Ecto is *approachable*. As database libraries go, Ecto is a newcomer, but it has a sense of history and builds on work that has come before. The query syntax was inspired by LINQ in the .NET framework. The migrations and relation syntax feel a lot like ActiveRecord. Depending on the libraries you've used, you're likely to find parts of Ecto that will make you feel at home. The Ecto developers have tried to bring the best of what has come before, while avoiding some of the known pitfalls. Hopefully, your progress through learning Ecto will be met with responses of "oh, this feels very familiar," and "wow, that solves a problem that's been bugging me for years!"

Second, Ecto is *explicit.* Like the Elixir language itself, Ecto avoids the "magic" that characterizes many other database libraries. Magic is a seductive characteristic. It appears to make everything easy and efficient, but only at first. Over time, those hundreds of decisions made on your behalf start to catch up with you, and you lose track of what's actually going on. When you work with Ecto, you have clarity: you know exactly when your app is talking to the database, and what it's saying. This is welcome news if you've ever diagnosed a sluggish application and discovered that your database library was making dozens or hundreds of requests that you weren't even aware of.

Finally, Ecto is *flexible.* Ecto doesn't lock you into one particular way of working with it. In fact, it's more accurate to think of Ecto as a suite of tools for database access, rather than a large-scale framework you need to adapt to. You can use some parts of Ecto and not others. You can use them in various combinations. And, perhaps most surprising, you can use parts of Ecto without a relational database. We'll see some examples of this later in the book.

Ecto Modules

Ecto's core functionality is contained in six main modules, and in Part I, we'll look at each of them in detail.

Later in this chapter, we'll start with Repo. Repo is the heart of Ecto and acts as a kind of proxy for your database. All communication to and from the database goes through Repo.

The Query module contains Ecto's powerful but elegant API for writing queries. Here you'll find everything you need to pull the data you want out of your database, and make precise changes.

A schema is a kind of map, from database tables to your code. The Schema module contains tools to help you create these maps with ease. The best part is Ecto schemas are very flexible—you're not locked into a simple one-to-one relationship between your tables and your structs. As you'll see, this allows for whole new levels of expressiveness when creating your data structures.

Many database layers have one or two kinds of change. Ecto understands that one size does not fit all, so it provides the *changeset:* a data structure that captures all aspects of making a change to your data. The Changeset module provides functions for creating and manipulating changesets, allowing you to structure your changes in a way that is safe, flexible, and easy to test.

You often need to coordinate several database changes simultaneously, where they must all succeed or fail together. The transaction function works great for simple cases, but the Multi module can handle even very complex cases while still keeping your code clean and testable.

Change happens. As your app grows and evolves, so too must the underlying database. Changing the structure of a database can be tricky, particularly when multiple developers are involved, but Migration helps you coordinate these changes so that everyone stays in sync.

We'll get started on our tour with the Repo module, but before we do that, we'll take a moment to set up a small sample application that uses Ecto. We'll use this app throughout the book as a playground to try out Ecto functions as we learn them.

How Ecto Is Organized

Under the hood, Ecto is actually two separate packages: ecto and ecto_sql. The ecto package contains some of the core data manipulation features that are useful even if you're not using a relational database. These include the Repo, Query, Schema, and Changeset modules (among others).

ecto_sql, on the other hand, contains modules specifically needed to communicate with relational databases. These include the various database-specific adapters, migrations, and so forth.

The ecto_sql package includes ecto as a dependency, so if you're using Ecto to work with a relational database, you just need to include ecto_sql in your dependencies, and you'll get ecto in the process. But if you're not working with a relational database and want to take advantage of the some of the data manipulation features that Ecto offers (validations, for example) you can include ecto rather than ecto_sql and your dependency tree will be a little lighter.

Setting Up the Sample App

To get a real feel for Ecto, you'll want to write and execute some code for yourself, and not just read about it. In Chapter 7, Adding Ecto to an Elixir Application Without Phoenix, on page 123 we walk through all the steps of how to add Ecto to an existing application, but for now, we want to make this as easy as possible.

We've created a small Elixir application with Ecto already installed and set up. This app is a very simple music database that you might use to keep track of your music collection. It's a standard Elixir mix project that comes with Ecto and sample data already baked in. All you need to do is download it, configure it to work with your local database, and you're ready to go. In this section, we'll walk you through the process.

To start, you'll need Elixir 1.5 or greater, and a database that can support Ecto 3 (we recommend Postgres, but you can also use MySQL). If you don't have Elixir installed, you can get it here.[1] Postgres can be downloaded here.[2]

Working with MySQL

Almost all of the code examples in this book work with both Postgres and MySQL, but Ecto does take advantage of a few features that are available only in Postgres, and we cover some of these features in the book. Whenever there's an example that behaves differently in the two databases, we'll make a note of it in the book text.

As of this writing, Ecto uses the mariaex package as its database driver for MySQL, but a new driver called myxql is currently under development. This will be the preferred driver as soon as Ecto 3.1 is released, so if you're working with MySQL and you have Ecto 3.1 or later, you may wish to modify your mix.exs and replace mariaex with myxql in your dependencies.

Once you are sure those two pieces are in place, download the code as described in Online Resources, on page xiii and unzip the file somewhere on your system. Then:

1) Run mix do deps.get, compile to download dependencies and compile the app.

2) In your favorite editor, open 'config/config.exs' and look at the section starting with:

```
config :music_db, MusicDB.Repo
```

These are the settings that the app will use to connect to your database, so double-check them to make sure they'll work. In particular, make sure the username and password are correct.

---

1. http://elixir-lang.org/install.html
2. https://www.postgresql.org/download

If you're a little confused as to what we're doing in here, don't worry; we'll be covering how this configuration works in the next section.

3) If you're using MySQL, you'll need to change the MusicDB.Repo module to use a different adapter. Open up lib/music_db/repo.ex and change the adapter: setting from Ecto.Adapters.Postgres to Ecto.Adapters.MySQL.

Once you've made the necessary changes, save the files, hop back over to your terminal window, and run

```
mix ecto.setup
```

This is an alias that we've created for our music_db app that wraps up three mix tasks into one command:

- mix ecto.create
- mix ecto.migrate
- mix run priv/repo/seeds.exs

These commands create the database, run all the migrations (which create the individual tables), and load the sample data, respectively. When this is done, you'll have a fully populated database, and you should see something like this:

```
Sample data successfully loaded.
```

You should be good to go at this point. To confirm, open up a mix console by typing iex -S mix. Once you're in, type in this line of code (this tells Ecto to fetch the number of records in the artists table):

```
MusicDB.Repo.aggregate("artists", :count, :id)
```

You should get a single integer in response (as of this writing, it should be 3, but it's possible we've added some data since the book was printed). If you see that, you're all set.

Running the Examples

To run the code snippets included in the book, you have two options.

You can open up an IEx session with iex -S mix as we did in the last section, and type or copy/paste the code directly into the console. This works great for one- or two-line examples.

For longer examples, the app has a built-in playground for you to try out code that might be too ambitious to type into the console. Just open up your editor and find the priv/repo/playground.exs file. Once you're there, find the play function—it's pretty well marked with a big PUT YOUR TEST CODE HERE in the comments.

Put whatever code you'd like into that function, then go back to your terminal. Exit out of your IEx session (if you're still in one), then type:

```
mix run priv/repo/playground.exs
```

This will execute the code in the play function and print the result.

If you find yourself typing something that feels too complicated for IEx, jump back into this file and code to your heart's content. You'll definitely want to do this for anything that uses the pipe operator (|>) across multiple lines, as this doesn't work correctly in IEx.

Resetting the Sample Data

As we work through the examples in the book, we'll be making lots of changes to the sample data that we installed earlier. Over time, our changes will mangle the data to the point where it's no longer usable. When that happens, it's time for a reset.

To get the data back to its pristine state, exit out of your IEx session (if you're in one) and run this command:

```
mix ecto.reset
```

This single command will drop the database, re-create it, and repopulate it with the original sample data. This should only take a couple of seconds, so it's a good idea to run it between sections of the book, just to make sure you're starting with a clean slate.

Data Model of the Sample App

The data model for this app is much simpler than what you would use for a real music database, but it should have enough to let us explore the major features of Ecto without having to wrap our heads around too much data modeling detail.

It contains four tables:

- artists
- albums
- tracks
- genres

You can probably guess the associations between the tables: an artist can have many albums, an album can have many tracks. Albums have a many-to-many relationship with genres as shown in the figure on page 9.

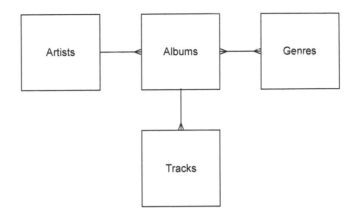

If you're curious about how Ecto created these tables, you can peek ahead to Chapter 6, Making Changes to Your Database, on page 101 where we cover migrations in detail, but you don't need to know that to get started.

All the code examples in Part I will work with this data model. We encourage you to keep your terminal open while you read so you can try out the examples as we go—you'll retain more if you actually get the Ecto code into your fingers.

The Repository Pattern

Now that we've got the sample app up and running, we're ready to begin our tour of Ecto. We're going to start with the big picture and take a look at Ecto's approach to database access. Ecto adopts the Repository pattern for accessing the underlying data store. Understanding this pattern will help make sense of Ecto's overall architecture, so let's take a quick look.

Open a mix session in the music_db app we set up in the last section: iex -S mix. Then type in the following lines of code (you don't have to enter the comments—that's just to help clarify what's going on):

priv/examples/getting_started_01.exs
```
alias MusicDB.{Repo, Artist}

# insert a record into the artists table
Repo.insert(%Artist{name: "Dizzy Gillespie"})

# retrieve the record
dizzy = Repo.get_by(Artist, name: "Dizzy Gillespie")

# make a change
Repo.update(Ecto.Changeset.change(dizzy, name: "John Birks Gillespie"))

# retrieve it again
dizzy = Repo.get_by(Artist, name: "John Birks Gillespie")

# delete it
Repo.delete(dizzy)
```

Notice that every time we want to do something with the database, we call a function in Repo. That's the repository pattern at work. The main characteristic of this pattern is the presence of a single module or class, called the Repository, through which all communication with the database passes. Your app code creates queries and submits them to the Repository, which in turn sends them across the wire to the database. The Repository also handles the response, and packages it up in a friendly way for your app to consume.

The Repository pattern is not unique to Ecto. Martin Fowler describes it in *Patterns of Enterprise Application Architecture,* as does Eric Evans in *Domain-Driven Design.* Implementations can differ slightly, and Ecto has its own unique take on the approach. The key point to bear in mind is that the Repository acts as a stand-in for your database, and it's the single point of contact—if you want to talk to the database, you talk to the Repository.

This is in sharp contrast to many other data access patterns, notably Active Record. In that pattern, communication with the database is more opaque. You simply perform operations on in-memory data structures, and the necessary SQL commands are silently dispatched and sent to database completely behind the scenes. With the Repository pattern, the database is front and center. With Active Record, it almost disappears.

Both patterns are viable options, and many excellent libraries have been built with both. But the Repository pattern is a great fit for a language like Elixir, which decouples data and behavior, and favors explicit behavior over implicit.

If you're new to the Repository pattern, Ecto may feel quite different at first, but over time, it will start to become second nature. You may even begin to wonder how you lived this long without it.

The Repo Module

Now that we've got a handle on what a Repository is, let's look at how it's implemented in Ecto. The Repo module is the heart of Ecto, and just about everything you do will touch Repo in some way. Repo is also quite powerful; as you're about to see, you can perform all of the classic CRUD operations (create, read, update, delete) using just the Repo module alone. The other modules in Ecto make these operations easier, but there's a lot you can do with just Repo.

Given its relationship to the Repository pattern, Repo contains a lot of functions you'd expect: get, insert, update, delete, and the like. What you might not expect is that you never call these functions directly. Instead, you create your own Repo module that lives in your app's codebase, then integrate Ecto.Repo's functions with Elixir's use macro. Let's see this in action.

In our sample project, open up lib/music_db/repo.ex and you'll see this:

```
lib/music_db/repo.ex
defmodule MusicDB.Repo do
  use Ecto.Repo,
    otp_app: :music_db,
    adapter: Ecto.Adapters.Postgres
end
```

This sets up the Repo module we'll use in our app. We can name it anything we'd like, but the convention is to use "Repo," so that's what we will use throughout this book. We then pull in the critical functions from Ecto.Repo with the use macro. This gives our module access to all the good stuff Ecto provides.

What exactly does "use" do?

 It's one of the tools, along with import and require, that Elixir provides to integrate code from other modules. use goes beyond simply including functions, and actually executes a specified block of code in the current context. You'll work with use quite a bit in Ecto. You don't need to know all the gory details, but if you're curious, check out the official documentation.[3]

The otp_app option is required. It tells Ecto where to find the configuration values it needs to connect to your database. You worked with these values in the previous section when you modified config/dev.exs to match your local database installation. Your version probably looks something like this:

```
config :music_db, MusicDB.Repo,
  database: "music_db",
  username: "postgres",
  password: "postgres",
  hostname: "localhost"
```

This is where the otp_app option comes into play. It tells Ecto to look here to find the values it needs to communicate with the database. Different database adapters may require different settings, so check the documentation to find out exactly what Ecto expects to see here.

In our example, we used separate values for these settings but it's possible to combine all of these into a single url parameter. The format for the URL should be ecto://USERNAME:PASSWORD@HOSTNAME/DATABASE_NAME. For our configuration, we could use this:

```
config :music_db, MusicDB.Repo,
  url: "ecto://postgres:postgres@localhost/music_db"
```

---

3.   https://hexdocs.pm/elixir/Kernel.html#use/2

Using a URL can simplify creating a secure configuration, as you can put all of the connection parameters into a single URL stored as an environment variable. But if you want to load the URL dynamically (and you should), you'll need to set that up elsewhere. We'll look at that in *Customizing Your Repo* later in this chapter.

Putting Our Repo to Work

As we saw earlier, Repo is the gateway to our database, and most of the functions in Repo map directly to standard CRUD operations. This makes Repo fairly small compared to some other Ecto modules: its one job is sending payloads back and forth to the database. But we can use this small handful of functions to create, read, update, and delete records. Let's try it.

Repo exposes a number of functions that allow us to interact with our database at a low level, even before we start setting up schemas. These functions are easy to spot because they end with "all": insert_all, update_all, delete_all, and just plain all for queries.

For example, our music app includes an artists table. Here's how we can insert a new record into that table:

```
priv/examples/getting_started_02.exs
alias MusicDB.Repo

Repo.insert_all("artists", [[name: "John Coltrane"]])
#=> {1, nil}
```

A Quick Note About alias

 We've added alias MusicDB.Repo to this example so that we can refer to Repo without its MusicDB namespace. This is a convention that we'll follow in the code throughout the book. To keep the examples concise, we won't be adding alias every time, but we've included several alias statements in the .iex.exs file included with the source code of this project, so you should be able to type (or copy) the code as written while you're working in IEx. If you're curious, you can peer into .iex.exs and see what it's doing for you. We'll also examine this file in detail in Chapter 15, Optimizing IEx for Ecto, on page 189.

In the last example, we were only setting the name field on our new record, but we could set other fields by including more keyword pairs:

```
Repo.insert_all("artists",
  [[name: "Sonny Rollins", inserted_at: DateTime.utc_now()]])
#=> {1, nil}
```

If we want to insert more than one record, we can just add another set of values inside the outer list:

```
Repo.insert_all("artists",
  [[name: "Max Roach", inserted_at: DateTime.utc_now()],
   [name: "Art Blakey", inserted_at: DateTime.utc_now()]])
#=> {2, nil}
```

In these examples, we specified the values using keyword lists, but you can also use maps. This snippet will do the exact same thing as the previous one:

```
Repo.insert_all("artists",
  [%{name: "Max Roach", inserted_at: DateTime.utc_now()},
   %{name: "Art Blakey", inserted_at: DateTime.utc_now()}])
#=> {2, nil}
```

To update records, we can use the update_all function:

```
Repo.update_all("artists", set: [updated_at: DateTime.utc_now()])
#=> {9, nil}
```

Here we use the set option to tell Ecto which fields and values we want to change, but update_all provides some other options for making changes:

- inc: This increments the given field by the given value; we can decrement by supplying a negative number

- push: This works on columns containing an array, and pushes the given value onto the end of the array

- pull: This also works on array columns—it removes the given value from the array

See the official documentation for more details on these options.[4]

If we want to delete a bunch of records, we can do that with delete_all. This example will remove all of the records from the tracks table:

```
Repo.delete_all("tracks")
#=> {33, nil}
```

If you just ran this command in IEx (and we hope you have), you just deleted all the records in the tracks table. Oops. But remember that you can restore all the app's sample data by exiting out of IEx and running mix ecto.reset on the command line.

---

4. https://hexdocs.pm/ecto/Ecto.Query.html#update/3-operators

Getting Values Back

In each of the examples we've seen so far, Ecto returns a tuple. This is the standard return value for the *_all functions. The first item in the tuple is the number of records affected by the operation. The second contains the values that we asked the database to return. We haven't been using that option so far, which is why we keep getting nil. Let's try it now.

The returning option lets us specify any values we'd like returned to us after the operation completes. This option takes a list of the field names we're interested in, and Ecto returns the values as a map. Note that this option works in Postgres, but not in MySQL.

To try this out, let's go back to inserting new records. When we first set up our database, we made the id column the primary key, and we asked the database to assign these IDs automatically. We can use returning to have Ecto show us the IDs after inserting the records:

```
priv/examples/getting_started_03.exs
Repo.insert_all("artists", [%{name: "Max Roach"},
  %{name: "Art Blakey"}], returning: [:id, :name])
#=> {2, [%{id: 12, name: "Max Roach"}, %{id: 13, name: "Art Blakey"}]}
```

As expected, we get a map for each record we inserted, and each map contains values for the two fields we asked for, id and name. This option works with any of the *all functions.

Executing Queries

At this point, you're probably starting to wonder about how to run queries. Inserting, updating, and deleting are all well and good, but queries are the real meat and potatoes of most database-backed applications, so how do we do that?

Ecto provides an elegant and powerful query interface in the Query module, and we'll be looking at that in detail in the next chapter. But it's worth pointing out that if you're a fan of using raw SQL for your queries, you have that option. The Ecto.Adapters.SQL module has a function called query that will take good old-fashioned SQL:

```
Ecto.Adapters.SQL.query(Repo, "select * from artists where id=1")
#=> {:ok,
#=>  %Postgrex.Result{
#=>    columns: ["id", "name", "birth_date", "death_date", "inserted_at",
#=>     "updated_at"],
#=>    command: :select,
#=>    connection_id: 3333,
```

```
#=>    messages: [],
#=>    num_rows: 1,
#=>    rows: [
#=>      [1, "Miles Davis", nil, nil, ~N[2018-1-05 23:32:31.000000],
#=>       ~N[2018-1-05 23:32:31.000000]]
#=>    ]
#=> }}
```

Ecto also makes this function available from Repo—this shortcut doesn't appear in the documentation for Repo but it's simpler to call:

```
Repo.query("select * from artists where id=1")
```

As you can see, the return value is a little hard to parse, and working with SQL in string form can get pretty clumsy and even unsafe, particularly as you start adding dynamic values. However, this approach can be useful when debugging, or if you want to run a quick SQL statement within an IEx session.

The Query module is much better suited for running queries, as you will soon see. Stay tuned.

Customizing Your Repo

For many projects, you won't need to do much to your Repo module. With that one use Ecto.Repo call, you'll have access to everything you need. But there may be times when you find yourself calling some particular Repo functions over and over with the same set of options, or maybe you'd like to add some behavior that Repo doesn't currently have. Fortunately, the Repo module you created is a plain old Elixir module just like any other, so it's possible to add customized behavior just by adding more functions.

For example, we might decide that we're going to be doing a lot of counting in our music app: how many albums we have, how many artists, and so forth. Getting the number of records in a table is fairly easy with Repo's aggregate function. Here's how we can see how many albums we have:

priv/examples/getting_started_05.exs
```
Repo.aggregate("albums", :count, :id)
#=> 5
```

This function gives us access to a number of aggregate functions supplied by the underlying database: count, avg, min, max, sum, and so on. To use this function, we just provide the name of the table we're interested in, the aggregate function we want to run, and which column to use. For count the column doesn't matter too much, but we'll use id because we know that each record will have one.

This function is simple enough, but if we know we'll be doing this often and want to be truly lazy, we can add a custom count function to our Repo module to save some typing. In the sample project, open lib/music_db/repo.ex and add this function:

```
def count(table) do
  aggregate(table, :count, :id)
end
```

If you've got an open IEx session, you can pick up this change by recompiling Repo with the r command:

```
iex(1)> r Repo
```

Now when we want to count the records in a table, we can just do this:

```
Repo.count("albums")
#=> 5
```

Even easier!

Another useful customization is adding an implementation of the init callback. This runs when Ecto first initializes and allows you to add or override configuration parameters. Earlier in the chapter we talked about loading a database connection URL from an environment variable. The init callback is where you'd want to do that:

```
def init(_, opts) do
  {:ok, Keyword.put(opts, :url, System.get_env("DATABASE_URL"))}
end
```

See the Repo documentation for more details.[5]

You may not find that you need to customize your Repo very often, but it's good to know that you can if you need to.

Wrapping Up

We have completed the first stop of our tour of Ecto. We looked at Ecto from a high level, we set up a sample app, and we learned about the Repository pattern and how it's implemented in Ecto. From there, we dove into the Repo module and started running a few basic CRUD operations. We are well on our way.

---

5. https://hexdocs.pm/ecto/Ecto.Repo.html#module-urls

Repo is powerful, but it's a blunt instrument, and Ecto has many other tools available to help us with our work. In particular, we noticed that running queries with raw SQL was rather clumsy. Ecto has a better option. Our next stop is the Query module, where we'll learn how to use Ecto's clean, elegant syntax to create queries ranging from the very simple to the very complex. Let's take a look.

## CHAPTER 2

Querying Your Database

For the next stop on our tour, we'll look at writing queries. Queries are an essential operation for writing database-backed applications, but, as we saw in the last chapter, writing queries with raw SQL was a little cumbersome. The Query module makes writing queries much easier, and it can handle just about anything you'd want to throw at it, from the very simple to the very complex.

In this chapter, we'll look at the Query module in detail. We'll start by examining Ecto's query syntax, and try our hand at writing some simple queries. From there, we'll look at writing more advanced queries using where and join. We'll then see how Ecto allows us to break up larger queries into smaller, reusable pieces with its composability features. We'll wrap up by applying what we've learned about queries to some of the Repo functions we learned about in the last chapter.

Before we begin, we want to take a moment to mention schemas. If you've worked with Ecto before, or even just browsed the documentation, you've probably seen queries written with Ecto schemas rather than with raw table names. We'll be covering schemas in depth in the next chapter, but for now, we'll write our queries without them. We have a couple reasons for this. First, we want to demonstrate that schemas aren't necessary for writing queries in Ecto (in fact, they sometimes get in the way). And second, we want you to focus your full attention on Ecto's query API, without having to keep track of how schemas work at the same time. After you've had some experience writing queries, adding schemas will make much more sense, and you'll have a better idea of when they help and when they don't.

With that in mind, make sure your terminal window is open, and let's get started.

Query Basics

Let's start with the basics. We'll take a quick look at Ecto's query syntax, then start writing some simple queries, including some that integrate user input.

The Query module uses Elixir macros to create a DSL (domain-specific language) that sits right in your Elixir code. The DSL syntax feels a lot like Elixir, but it's a little more fluid and makes writing queries feel more natural.

For example, here's a SQL query based on the data model in our sample app. You can run this in a Postgres console to see what it does:

priv/examples/query_01.exs
```
SELECT t.id, t.title, a.title
  FROM tracks t
  JOIN albums a ON t.album_id = a.id
  WHERE t.duration > 900;
```

And here's that same query written in Ecto:

```
query = from t in "tracks",
  join: a in "albums", on: t.album_id == a.id,
  where: t.duration > 900,
  select: [t.id, t.title, a.title]
```

Even if you don't understand everything these queries do, you can see the similarities. Most of the keywords are the same, and the expressions are nearly identical.

Ecto provides two ways to compose queries. The preceding example uses the *keyword syntax*, but you can also use the *macro syntax*, which leans heavily on Elixir's |> operator. Here's the same query written using the macro syntax:

```
query = "tracks"
|> join(:inner, [t], a in "albums", on: t.album_id == a.id)
|> where([t,a], t.duration > 900)
|> select([t,a], [t.id, t.title, a.title])
```

Some developers prefer this approach, as the pipe operator makes the code feel more Elixirish, but it's also more verbose. We'll be using the keyword syntax throughout this book, but Ecto's documentation for the Query API usually includes examples for both. You can experiment and see what feels better to you.

To get our feet wet, we'll start by writing a very simple query. Let's just grab all of the values from the name column in the artists table:

```
query = from "artists", select: [:name]
#=> #Ecto.Query<from a in "artists", select: [:name]>
```

This snippet creates an Ecto.Query struct, which we then assign to the mundanely named variable query.

As the output of the statement shows, all we have at this point is a simple data structure: the database itself hasn't been touched. When it's time to run the query, Ecto will take this data structure and convert it into a SQL statement for us. We can see the statement it'll generate with the Ecto.Adapters.SQL.to_sql function:

```
query = from "artists", select: [:name]
Ecto.Adapters.SQL.to_sql(:all, Repo, query)
#=> {"SELECT a0.\"name\" FROM \"artists\" AS a0", []}
```

This function takes three parameters: an atom representing the Repo function you plan on using (:all, :delete_all, or :update_all), your Repo module, and the query.

Although it's not documented, you can also call this function directly from Repo, which simplifies the code a bit:

```
query = from "artists", select: [:name]
Repo.to_sql(:all, query)
```

to_sql comes in handy when queries produce unexpected results, as it helps you see exactly what's going on under the hood.

Even after generating the SQL, we still haven't sent anything to the database. To run the query, we have to hand it off to our repo (recall that with the Repository pattern, the repo handles all database communication). We'll do this with the Repo.all function we saw briefly in the last chapter:

```
query = from "artists", select: [:name]
Repo.all(query)
#=> [%{name: "Miles Davis"}, %{name: "Bill Evans"},
#=> %{name: "Bobby Hutcherson"}]
```

Now we've involved the database, and Ecto has returned a list of maps, one for each record in our result set. We only specified one column in our select, so each map just has one item: the name value we asked for.

Let's look closely at what's going on. As you might've guessed, from is part of the Ecto.Query module, and the preceding example is a shorthand version of this:

```
query = Ecto.Query.from("artists", select: [:name])
```

With the full module name and the added parentheses, the query looks a little less mysterious. It seems that we're really just calling a function named from that returns a Query struct. But the real story is that from is a macro, and, as we'll see, this allows Ecto to provide an extra level of expressiveness that you don't get with a standard function call.

Most developers omit the parenthesis when writing queries, and import the from function so that it can be called without the full module name. These two shortcuts add an almost-like-SQL feel to queries—we'll follow both of those conventions throughout the book.

What exactly is a macro?

 In a nutshell, a macro is code that writes code. Macros allow developers to extend the Elixir language by writing specialized functions that are evaluated before the rest of the code is compiled. This means that there's an extra level of pre-processing that can happen with macros that doesn't happen with regular functions. Ecto uses macros to provide some syntactic sugar that bridges the gap between Elixir and SQL. At compile time, Ecto's query syntax is transformed into plain Elixir code, which does the same thing, but doesn't look as nice. You can read more about macros in the official Elixir guide.[1]

The Ecto.Query.from/1 macro is the starting point for all Ecto queries. It has one required parameter: the table that we want to query, and a number of optional parameters that refine the query. For now, we must provide the select option to specify which columns we'd like Ecto to return. If we don't, Ecto will complain:

```
query = from "artists"
Repo.all(query)
#=> ** (Ecto.QueryError) ...
```

This error makes it seem like select should be a required parameter, not optional. But this is because we haven't started working with schemas yet. When we get to the Schema module in the next chapter, we'll see how to make the select parameter go away.

If you're using prefixes in your database, you can specify them in your query with the prefix: keyword:

```
query = from "artists", prefix: "public", select: [:name]
```

The option behaves differently depending on the database you're using. For PostgreSQL, this value refers to the schema where the table is located, and defaults to "public." For MySQL, the value refers to the name of the database, and defaults to the value you specified in your Repo configuration.

---

1.   http://elixir-lang.org/getting-started/meta/macros.html

Not all apps will need to take advantage of this feature, but Ecto supports it if you need it. The prefix can be set for the entire query, or just for specific parts. See the documentation[2] for more details and examples.

Refining Our Results with where

Now that we know some of the query basics, we'll start filtering the results with the where option. We'll also see how to integrate dynamic input into queries (user input, for example), and how Ecto protects you from SQL injection attacks.

To start, we're going to look up the id and name for the artist named "Bill Evans":

```
priv/examples/query_02.exs
q = from "artists", where: [name: "Bill Evans"], select: [:id, :name]
Repo.all(q)
#=> [%{id: 2, name: "Bill Evans"}]
```

Great, that works. We added the where option and gave it a list of values to look for (in this case, just the name column). But what if we wanted to query for a dynamic value, say a value we got from the user? You might be tempted to do something like this:

```
artist_name = "Bill Evans"
q = from "artists", where: [name: artist_name], select: [:id, :name]
```

It seems like that should work. We're just passing a one-element keyword list to the where parameter, and artist_name is just a plain old Elixir variable—but we'll get an error:

```
** (Ecto.Query.CompileError) variable `artist_name` is not a valid query
expression. Variables need to be explicitly interpolated in queries with ^
...
```

Let's take a deeper look to see what's going on.

Recall that much of Ecto's query syntax is implemented using macros, so the rules are a little different. In this case, the error message tells us what we need to do. We need to alert the macro that we're using an expression that needs evaluating by adding ^ (referred to as "the pin operator"). If we prepend our variable with that operator, we're back in business:

```
artist_name = "Bill Evans"
q = from "artists", where: [name: ^artist_name], select: [:id, :name]
#=> #Ecto.Query<from a in "artists", where: a.name == ^"Bill Evans",
#=> select: [:id, :name]>
```

---

2. https://hexdocs.pm/ecto/Ecto.Query.html#module-query-prefix

You can use any valid Elixir expression with the pin operator. If you just need to evaluate a variable, putting the pin operator in front is all you need. But if you've got a more complex expression, you need to wrap it in parentheses, like this: ^("Bill" <> " Evans")

Protecting Against SQL Injection

The pin operator performs another critical job: it protects you from SQL injection attacks. When Ecto converts the Query struct into a SQL statement, any values added by the pin operator become parameterized values.

You can verify this by using to_sql to look at the query:

```
priv/examples/query_03.exs
artist_name = "Bill Evans"
q = from "artists", where: [name: ^artist_name], select: [:id, :name]
Ecto.Adapters.SQL.to_sql(:all, Repo, q)
#=> {"SELECT a0.\"id\", a0.\"name\" FROM \"artists\" AS a0
#=> WHERE (a0.\"name\" = $1)", ["Bill Evans"]}
```

Instead of dropping the value of artist_name directly into the generated SQL, Ecto does the right thing and turns it into a query parameter. You will likely write a lot a queries that involve user-supplied input, so it's good to know that Ecto is looking out for you.

Dynamic Values and Their Types

When working with dynamic values, you have to give some thought to data types. Take a look at this example:

```
priv/examples/query_04.exs
artist_id = 1
q = from "artists", where: [id: ^artist_id], select: [:name]
Repo.all(q)
#=> [%{name: "Miles Davis"}]
```

That works fine. artist_id is an integer and the id column in our Postgres database is an integer, so the value goes across the wire with no problem. If the value came in as a string, however, we'd have trouble:

```
artist_id = "1"
q = from "artists", where: [id: ^artist_id], select: [:name]
Repo.all(q)
#=> ** (DBConnection.EncodeError) Postgrex expected an integer
#=> in -2147483648..2147483647 that can be encoded/cast to
#=> type "int4", got "1". Please make sure the value you
#=> are passing matches the definition in your table or
#=> in your query or convert the value accordingly.
```

Not good. In this case, we need to instruct Ecto to make the type conversion for us, using Ecto's type function:

```
artist_id = "1"
q = from "artists", where: [id: type(^artist_id, :integer)], select: [:name]
Repo.all(q)
#=> [%{name: "Miles Davis"}]
```

If this mucking about with types seems overly tedious, fear not: the Schema module will come to our rescue in the next chapter.

Query Bindings

At this point, we've gotten our feet wet with queries, and we can handle dynamic values as well as hardcoded values. Now let's start exploring some of the query expressions that Ecto provides, so we can start writing more complex queries.

The where expression we've been using so far has been very simple. As we've seen, it just checks for equality:

priv/examples/query_05.exs
```
q = from "artists", where: [name: "Bill Evans"], select: [:id, :name]
```

You might well wonder if you could write the query like this:

```
q = from "artists", where: name == "Bill Evans", select: [:id, :name]
```

You can't. The trouble is that Ecto can't easily figure out what name is supposed to be. A variable? A function or macro defined elsewhere? We need a way to tell Ecto that name is a column in our artists table. We can do this with *query bindings*.

You create a query binding by using in along with the usual from. It works a lot like table aliases in SQL and effectively gives you a variable for referring to your table throughout your query. Our problematic query can be rewritten like this:

```
q = from a in "artists", where: a.name == "Bill Evans", select: [:id, :name]
```

In this example, a becomes the binding for the artists table, and we can use it throughout the query to refer to the columns in that table. You can use any valid Elixir variable name for the binding. We chose a just to keep it short and sweet, but any name will work.

Query Expressions

With query bindings in our toolbox, our where clauses can get a lot more sophisticated. Ecto provides a long list of functions that you can use with where and other query keywords. These are documented in detail in the Ecto.Query.API module, but here are a few examples to give you an idea of what's possible:

```
priv/examples/query_06.exs
# like statements
q = from a in "artists", where: like(a.name, "Miles%"), select: [:id, :name]

# checking for null
q = from a in "artists", where: is_nil(a.name), select: [:id, :name]

# checking for not null
q = from a in "artists", where: not is_nil(a.name), select: [:id, :name]

# date comparison - this finds artists added more than 1 year ago
q = from a in "artists", where: a.inserted_at < ago(1, "year"),
  select: [:id, :name]
```

For a complete list of all the available expressions, see the documentation for Ecto.Query.API.[3]

Inserting Raw SQL

Ecto's query API gives you just about everything you need to write even very complex queries, but you might have cases where your database exposes some specialized function that Ecto doesn't support. The fragment function gives you an escape hatch for writing bits of raw SQL that get inserted verbatim into the query.

Here we use fragment so we can call the Postgres lower function:

```
priv/examples/query_07.exs
q = from a in "artists",
  where: fragment("lower(?)", a.name) == "miles davis",
  select: [:id, :name]
```

We can use to_sql again to see exactly how Ecto works this into the rest of the query:

```
q = from a in "artists",
  where: fragment("lower(?)", a.name) == "miles davis",
  select: [:id, :name]
Ecto.Adapters.SQL.to_sql(:all, Repo, q)
#=> {"SELECT a0.\"id\", a0.\"name\" FROM \"artists\" AS a0
#=> WHERE (lower(a0.\"name\") = 'miles davis')", []}
```

If this is something you think you'll be using a lot, you can extend Ecto's query API by adding your own macro and importing it into your module:

---

3. https://hexdocs.pm/ecto/Ecto.Query.API.html

```
defmacro lower(arg) do
  quote do: fragment("lower(?)", unquote(arg))
end
```

Then the query could be rewritten like this:

```
q = from a in "artists",
  where: lower(a.name) == "miles davis",
  select: [:id, :name]
```

For more details on this approach, see the documentation for the fragment function[4].

Combining Results with union and union_all

To combine results of different queries, SQL provides the UNION operator. We can perform union queries in Ecto by adding the union: option to our queries. For this to work, the two queries need to have result sets with the same column names and data type.

Here's how we can use union: to get the titles of all our albums and tracks:

```
priv/examples/query_08.exs
tracks_query = from t in "tracks", select: t.title
union_query = from a in "albums", select: a.title,
  union: ^tracks_query
Repo.all(union_query)
#=> ["Without a Song", "Gary's Theme", "Miles", "Kind Of Blue", ...]
```

With union the database will filter the results so that they only contain unique rows. Depending on your database, this can add quite a bit of overhead. If you're certain that your results won't contain duplicates (or you don't care if they do), you can use union_all to generate a more efficient query:

```
tracks_query = from t in "tracks", select: t.title
union_query = from a in "albums", select: a.title,
  union_all: ^tracks_query
Repo.all(union_query)
#=> ["Without a Song", "Gary's Theme", "Miles", "Kind Of Blue", ...]
```

If you're familiar with the UNION operator, you're probably wondering if Ecto supports INTERSECT and EXCEPT, and the answer is yes. We can use intersect: to get a list of album titles that are also track titles:

```
tracks_query = from t in "tracks", select: t.title
intersect_query = from a in "albums", select: a.title,
  intersect: ^tracks_query
```

---

4.   https://hexdocs.pm/ecto/Ecto.Query.API.html#fragment/1

And we can use except: to get a list of album titles that are *not* also track titles:

```
tracks_query = from t in "tracks", select: t.title
except_query = from a in "albums", select: a.title,
  except: ^tracks_query
```

As with union: and union_all:, Ecto provides intersect_all: and except_all: when you're not concerned about potential duplicates.

Ordering and Grouping

SQL allows you to be specific about how your results are ordered. You can also group result rows together, which comes in pretty handy when you're trying to get counts in your results. The order by and group by expressions in SQL are available in Ecto via the order_by and group_by keywords. Let's see how those work.

If we wanted a list of all of artists in alphabetical order, we can use order_by like this:

```
priv/examples/query_08.exs
q = from a in "artists", select: [a.name], order_by: a.name
Repo.all(q)
#=> [["Bill Evans"], ["Bobby Hutcherson"], ["Miles Davis"]]
```

order_by returns the results in ascending order by default, but you can change this with the desc: keyword:

```
q = from a in "artists", select: [a.name], order_by: [desc: a.name]
Repo.all(q)
#=> [["Miles Davis"], ["Bobby Hutcherson"], ["Bill Evans"]]
```

You can also order by multiple columns by providing a list of column names to order_by. As happens when working with raw SQL, the results will be sorted by the first column provided to order_by, then by the second, and so on. In this next query, we'll get all tracks from our database, and we'll sort first by album_id and then by index. The result will show all of the tracks of each album, in per-album order:

```
q = from t in "tracks", select: [t.album_id, t.title, t.index],
  order_by: [t.album_id, t.index]
Repo.all(q)
#=> [[1, "So What", 1], [1, "Freddie Freloader", 2], [1, "Blue In Green", 3],
#=> [1, "All Blues", 4], [1, "Flamenco Sketches", 5],
#=> [2, "If I Were A Bell", 1], [2, "Stella By Starlight", 2],
#=> [2, "Walkin'", 3], [2, "Miles", 4], [2, "No Blues", 5], ... ]
```

You can sort specific columns in ascending or descending order by adding asc: and desc:

```
q = from t in "tracks", select: [t.album_id, t.title, t.index],
  order_by: [desc: t.album_id, asc: t.index]
Repo.all(q)
#=> [[5, "Anton's Ball", 1], [5, "The Moontrane", 2], [5, "Farallone", 3],
#=> [5, "Song Of Songs", 4], [4, "Come Rain Or Come Shine", 1], ... ]
```

By providing album_id as the first item to order_by, the tracks come back grouped by album. Then, within each of those groups, the tracks are sorted by the index value. If we reversed our order_by columns, we'd get all the tracks with index 1 first, then index 2, and so on:

```
q = from t in "tracks", select: [t.album_id, t.title, t.index],
  order_by: [t.index, t.album_id]
Repo.all(q)
#=> [[1, "So What", 1], [2, "If I Were A Bell", 1],
#=> [3, "B Minor Waltz (for Ellaine)", 1], [4, "Come Rain Or Come Shine", 1],
#=> [5, "Anton's Ball", 1], [1, "Freddie Freloader", 2],
#=> [2, "Stella By Starlight", 2], [3, "You Must Believe In Spring", 2],
#=> [4, "Autumn Leaves", 2], [5, "The Moontrane", 2], ...
```

When using order, you should give some thought to columns that might contain NULL. The default behavior varies between different databases: some put the NULL values first, others put them last. If you want to control where they appear, you can specify the ordering using :asc_nulls_last, :asc_nulls_first, :desc_nulls_last, or :desc_nulls_first (note that MySQL currently does not support these options):

```
q = from t in "tracks", select: [t.album_id, t.title, t.index],
  order_by: [desc: t.album_id, asc_nulls_first: t.index]
Repo.all(q)
#=> [[5, "Anton's Ball", 1], [5, "The Moontrane", 2], [5, "Farallone", 3],
#=> [5, "Song Of Songs", 4], [4, "Come Rain Or Come Shine", 1], ... ]
```

Let's say we wanted to get the total length of each album. We're going to need to look at the duration column of each track, but we don't actually want to see each individual track: we just want to see a single result for each album. When you want to collapse rows together like this, the group_by keyword is your friend. Here's how you can do it:

```
q = from t in "tracks", select: [t.album_id, sum(t.duration)],
  group_by: t.album_id
```

The group_by value tells Ecto that even though we're selecting across the tracks table, we only want one row for each album. In our select, we're grabbing the album_id (which we have to have if we want to include it in our group_by), and we use the sum function from Ecto.Query.API to add all the duration values together. The result looks like this:

```
Repo.all(q)
#=> [[4, 2540], [1, 2619], [5, 3057], [3, 3456], [2, 4491]]
```

Duration values are in seconds, so you'd need to do a little math to translate that into minutes and seconds.

Let's say we wanted to refine this further and only return the albums whose total length is longer than one hour (3600 seconds). A where clause won't help us here: that would only limit the records that get included in the duration counts. What we want is something like a where clause we can apply *after* we've totaled up the track lengths. And that's exactly what the having clause is for.

We'll take the same query and add having to include only the results that have a total duration longer than 3600 seconds:

```
q = from t in "tracks", select: [t.album_id, sum(t.duration)],
  group_by: t.album_id,
having: sum(t.duration) > 3600
Repo.all(q)
#=> [[2, 4491]]
```

That worked. However, the results would be a little more useful if we could see the album name, rather than the ID. The trouble is that the album name is in the albums table and this query only touches the tracks table. Read on to find out how to reach over to other tables and grab the values you need.

Working with Joins

Our queries have gotten more complex and expressive with the addition of the where option and all of the functions that can be used within it. But so far, we've only been working with one table at a time. When we need to query across multiple tables at once, we'll need *joins*. In this section, we'll see how to add joins to our queries, and also learn how to change our select option to make results from multiple columns easier to read.

What's a join?

 The term "join" comes from SQL. It's a feature of the language that allows you to combine data from two or more tables within the same query. Joins come in many different flavors, depending on how you want to filter the data coming from the different tables. If you need a primer on joins (or even a refresher), the SQL-Join website provides some detailed examples.[5]

To play with joins, we'll try a more ambitious query. We'll look up all the tracks in our database that are longer than 15 minutes, and the albums that they belong to.

---

5.   http://www.sql-join.com

This query is going to touch two different tables: tracks and albums. As you may recall, the tracks table has the foreign key album_id, which corresponds to the id column in the albums table, so we'll use those columns as a basis for our join. We'll use the query bindings we learned about in the last section to help us make sure we're referring to the right column in the right table.

To create the join, we'll use the join keyword to specify the table, and the on keyword to specify the column. The query bindings we learned about in the last chapter make it clear which table we're working with in each part of the expression:

priv/examples/query_09.exs
```
q = from t in "tracks", join: a in "albums", on: t.album_id == a.id
```

From there, we can add a where clause to find the very long tracks:

```
q = from t in "tracks",
  join: a in "albums", on: t.album_id == a.id,
  where: t.duration > 900,
  select: [a.title, t.title]
Repo.all(q)
#=> [["Cookin' At The Plugged Nickel", "No Blues"],
#=> ["Cookin' At The Plugged Nickel", "If I Were A Bell"]]
```

This works, but the result is a little hard to read. We can clean things up by changing our select statement. Instead of expressing the select as a list of columns, we can provide a map. Ecto will then return the result as list of maps, each using the structure we provide:

```
q = from t in "tracks",
  join: a in "albums", on: t.album_id == a.id,
  where: t.duration > 900,
  select: %{album: a.title, track: t.title}
Repo.all(q)
#=> [%{album: "Cookin' At The Plugged Nickel", track: "No Blues"},
#=> %{album: "Cookin' At The Plugged Nickel", track: "If I Were A Bell"}]
```

That's a little nicer.

You can apply the prefix: keyword to your join statements, if you need to query across different database schemas. If our tracks table used one prefix, and albums another, we could write the query like this:

```
q = from t in "tracks", prefix: "public",
  join: a in "albums", prefix: "private",
  on: t.album_id == a.id, where: t.duration > 900,
  select: %{album: a.title, track: t.title}
```

By default, the join macro performs an *inner join*, but other flavors of joins are available as well: left_join, right_join, cross_join, and full_join.

What if we needed to include more than one join in our query? Fortunately, Elixir's keyword lists allow you to specify the same keyword more than once, so adding more joins is simply a matter of adding more join and on options. If we wanted to include the artist name in our query, we could just do this:

```
q = from t in "tracks",
  join: a in "albums", on: t.album_id == a.id,
  join: ar in "artists", on: a.artist_id == ar.id,
  where: t.duration > 900,
  select: %{album: a.title, track: t.title, artist: ar.name}
Repo.all(q)
#=> [%{album: "Cookin' At The Plugged Nickel", artist: "Miles Davis",
#=> track: "If I Were A Bell"},
#=> %{album: "Cookin' At The Plugged Nickel", artist: "Miles Davis",
#=> track: "No Blues"}]
```

Using this pattern, you could add as many joins as you needed.

Composing Queries

With the addition of join we can start doing some larger and more detailed queries. This is a good time to look at one of the features of Query that simplifies working with complicated queries: composability. Ecto allows us to break up large queries into smaller pieces that can be reassembled at will. This makes them easier to work with, and allows you to re-use parts of queries in more than one place. This next section will show you exactly how to do that, and along the way, you'll learn a little bit more about how queries are constructed under the hood.

Let's say that we wanted to look up all of the albums by Miles Davis. Using joins, this query is straightforward:

```
priv/examples/query_10.exs
q = from a in "albums",
  join: ar in "artists", on: a.artist_id == ar.id,
  where: ar.name == "Miles Davis",
  select: [a.title]
Repo.all(q)
#=> [["Cookin' At The Plugged Nickel"], ["Kind Of Blue"]]
```

Now let's say that somewhere else in our code, we wanted a list of the tracks on those albums, and not just the album titles. We'd have to rewrite the query to look like this:

```
q = from a in "albums",
  join: ar in "artists", on: a.artist_id == ar.id,
  join: t in "tracks", on: t.album_id == a.id,
  where: ar.name == "Miles Davis",
  select: [t.title]
```

This is almost identical to the first query. We just added a join and changed the select. It would be nice if we could reuse the parts that are the same. It turns out we can, but to help understand how to do that, let's zoom in on what's going on with the from...in... clause we've been using.

So far, we've always been using strings on the right side of the in expression (for example, from a in "albums"). That string has always represented the name of a table in our database. But the in expression is actually looking for something broader than that: it's looking for any data type that has implemented the Ecto.Queryable protocol.

What's a protocol?

 Elixir uses protocols to define a behavior that can work with more than one datatype. A good example is Enumerable. Enumerable defines functions like count and member, and any data type that provides definitions for those functions can be used in any function that expects Enumerable. Protocols are the basis for using polymorphism in Elixir. For more details, see the section on protocols in the official Elixir guide.[6]

The Ecto.Queryable protocol specifies only one function that needs to be implemented: to_query. So you can think of Queryable as "a thing that can be queried."

As we've seen, Ecto provides an implementation for the String type, which is what we've been using so far. But it also provides an implementation for the Ecto.Query struct. This means that in can accept another query, not just a string. You can create one query and pass it along to another query for further refinement. And this is how we'll solve the reuse problem we ran into earlier.

Extracting Parts of Queries

With this knowledge in hand, let's return to our two similar queries, and see how we can break them down.

First, let's extract out the parts that are identical into a separate Query. Both queries refer to albums by Miles Davis, so we can break that logic out into its own query:

---

6. http://elixir-lang.org/getting-started/protocols.html

```
priv/examples/query_11.exs
albums_by_miles = from a in "albums",
  join: ar in "artists", on: a.artist_id == ar.id,
  where: ar.name == "Miles Davis"
```

In its current form, this is not complete—it's missing the select expression. If we tried to pass this to Repo.all, Ecto would complain. But recall that building a query is separate from actually running it. It's safe to create this as an incomplete query, then build on it later.

To make our first query that just fetches the album titles, we use our albums_by_miles query, and add select:

```
album_query = from a in albums_by_miles, select: a.title
#=> #Ecto.Query<from a0 in "albums", join: a1 in "artists",
#=>   on: a0.artist_id == a1.id, where: a1.name == "Miles Davis",
#=>   select: a0.title>
```

This works just like the other queries we've written, but instead of passing a table name to in we pass another query. Ecto takes that original query, then adds the select we've provided here. When we run the new query, the result is what we'd expect:

```
album_query = from a in albums_by_miles, select: a.title
Repo.all(album_query)
#=> ["Cookin' At The Plugged Nickel", "Kind Of Blue"]
```

You might be wondering what happens to the query bindings when a query is built up like this. The query bindings are still available, but they must be referred to in the same order that they first appeared. Let's take another look at our initial query:

```
albums_by_miles = from a in "albums",
  join: ar in "artists", on: a.artist_id == ar.id,
  where: ar.name == "Miles Davis"
```

We defined the a binding first, at the beginning of the from call, then later defined the ar binding in the join. This will be the order that Ecto will expect if the query is used again.

As it happens, we don't need the artists binding in the second query, but if we did, that binding would have to appear after the albums binding:

```
album_query = from [a,ar] in albums_by_miles, select: a.title
```

This wouldn't work:

```
album_query = from [ar,a] in albums_by_miles, select: a.title
```

The important thing to remember is that when composing queries, *binding order is preserved.* The upside of this arrangement is that the binding names can be changed, and you don't have to refer to any bindings you don't need. This is valid:

```
album_query = from albums in albums_by_miles, select: albums.title
```

Here we renamed the a binding from the original query to albums and we ignored the second binding (artists) because we don't need it.

Now let's look at how we can reuse the albums_by_miles query to get the tracks:

```
track_query = from a in albums_by_miles,
  join: t in "tracks", on: a.id == t.album_id,
  select: t.title
```

Here we take the same albums_by_miles query, but this time we add a join and an entirely different select.

Putting it all together, it looks like this:

```
albums_by_miles = from a in "albums",
  join: ar in "artists", on: a.artist_id == ar.id,
  where: ar.name == "Miles Davis"
album_query = from a in albums_by_miles, select: a.title
miles_albums = Repo.all(album_query)
track_query = from a in albums_by_miles,
  join: t in "tracks", on: a.id == t.album_id,
  select: t.title
miles_tracks = Repo.all(track_query)
```

Breaking queries into smaller pieces has a number of advantages. Smaller queries are easier to manage and easier to comprehend when reading unfamiliar code. They also make your queries more reusable.

Working with Named Bindings

With a small query like the one we just used, keeping track of the query bindings wasn't too difficult. The query composition spanned a small section of code, and we only had two bindings. But with a more complex query that's spread over a wider area, it could be tough to remember which binding needs to go where.

To help alleviate this problem, Ecto allows you to assign specific names to bindings that it saves throughout the life of the query. Let's look at how this works.

To create a named binding, you use the as: keyword. You can add this to the from call, or to any of the join options. Here's how we could rewrite our last query with named bindings:

```
priv/examples/query_11.exs
albums_by_miles = from a in "albums", as: :albums,
  join: ar in "artists", as: :artists,
  on: a.artist_id == ar.id, where: ar.name == "Miles Davis"
```

The as: needs to come immediately after from and join: and you must use atoms for binding names—strings are not allowed. This won't work:

```
albums_by_miles = from a in "albums", as: "albums",
  join: ar in "artists", as: "artists",
  on: a.artist_id == ar.id, where: ar.name == "Miles Davis"
#=> ** (Ecto.Query.CompileError) `as` must be a compile time atom...
```

To use the named binding in another query, you add the name to the beginning of the from call:

```
album_query = from [albums: a] in albums_by_miles, select: a.title
```

Here we're assigning the albums binding to the shorter name a. The a will only be available within this query statement, but we can reuse albums anywhere we reuse the query.

If we wanted to use the artists binding as well, we could add it to the list at the beginning of the from call. And in this case, we wouldn't have to worry about the binding order:

```
album_query = from [artists: ar, albums: a] in albums_by_miles,
  select: [a.title, ar.name]
```

Here we listed the artists binding first, even though it appears second in our original. With positional bindings, this would break our query. But with named bindings, we can specify the bindings in any order, and even eliminate bindings we don't need.

If you need to find out if a given query has a named binding, you can use the has_named_binding? function:

```
albums_by_miles = from a in "albums", as: :albums,
  join: ar in "artists", as: :artists,
  on: a.artist_id == ar.id, where: ar.name == "Miles Davis"
has_named_binding?(albums_by_miles, :albums)
#=> true
```

Named bindings are a convenience and you don't need to use them all the time. If you only have a couple of bindings, they may not be worth the extra typing required to use them. But if your query contains joins across several tables, and you're composing the query over a large section of code, named bindings can help simplify your query writing.

Composing Queries with Functions

One of the critical superpowers of Ecto is the ability to make queries from composable functions. This makes the query fragments reusable, and substantially improves readability.

For example, with just a slight tweak, we can take the albums_by_miles query we've been working with and put it into a function that will create a query for any artist's name:

```
priv/examples/query_12.exs
def albums_by_artist(artist_name) do
  from a in "albums",
    join: ar in "artists", on: a.artist_id == ar.id,
    where: ar.name == ^artist_name
end

albums_by_bobby = albums_by_artist("Bobby Hutcherson")
```

We could make that function even more flexible by allowing it to receive the target of the from statement, rather than hard-coding it to "albums":

```
def by_artist(query, artist_name) do
  from a in query,
    join: ar in "artists", on: a.artist_id == ar.id,
    where: ar.name == ^artist_name
end

albums_by_bobby = by_artist("albums", "Bobby Hutcherson")
```

With this change, we can now connect the output of this function to other queries. Earlier, we wrote an album query that used join to find albums with long tracks. Let's extract out that logic:

```
def with_tracks_longer_than(query, duration) do
  from a in query,
    join: t in "tracks", on: t.album_id == a.id,
    where: t.duration > ^duration,
    distinct: true
end
```

Now we can combine those queries into one using the pipe operator. Here's how we could find the albums by Miles Davis with tracks longer than 12 minutes:

```
q =
  "albums"
  |> by_artist("Miles Davis")
  |> with_tracks_longer_than(720)
```

Of course, this query is not complete without a select. We can put that into a function as well:

```
def title_only(query) do
  from a in query, select: a.title
end
q =
  "albums"
  |> by_artist("Miles Davis")
  |> with_tracks_longer_than(720)
  |> title_only

Repo.all(q)
#=> ["Cookin' At The Plugged Nickel"]
```

By breaking the query into separate components, and moving those components into functions, we've improved the readability of our code, and started to build up a collection of query fragments that we can reuse in any number of combinations. This is a common practice among Ecto developers, and when we look at schemas in the next chapter, we'll see that schema modules are an ideal place to put functions that generate queries. More on that soon.

Combining Queries with or_where

By default, Ecto combines where clauses with AND. Let's take two different query fragments, both of which use where on the name column of artists and see what happens when they're put together. First, we have a query that looks for albums by Miles Davis:

```
priv/examples/query_13.exs
albums_by_miles = from a in "albums",
  join: ar in "artists", on: a.artist_id == ar.id,
  where: ar.name == "Miles Davis"
```

Next, we build on that query, and add another where statement on the artist name. But this time, the name is "Bobby Hutcherson":

```
q = from [a,ar] in albums_by_miles,
  where: ar.name == "Bobby Hutcherson",
  select: a.title
```

We can use to_sql to see how Ecto combines these two queries:

```
Repo.to_sql(:all, q)
#=> {"SELECT a0.\"title\" FROM \"albums\" AS a0
#=> INNER JOIN \"artists\" AS a1
#=> ON a0.\"artist_id\" = a1.\"id\"
#=> WHERE (a1.\"name\" = 'Miles Davis')
#=> AND (a1.\"name\" = 'Bobby Hutcherson')", []}
```

As you might have guessed, the two where clauses are combined via AND, resulting in a query that looks for albums associated with both Miles Davis and Bobby Hutcherson. Given our current data model, that's not going to return any results.

But what if we wanted to do an "or" query, and get the albums that were either by Miles Davis or Bobby Hutcherson? If we put this into one query, we can use the or macro supplied by the query API:

```
q = from a in "albums",
  join: ar in "artists", on: a.artist_id == ar.id,
  where: ar.name == "Miles Davis" or ar.name == "Bobby Hutcherson",
  select: %{artist: ar.name, album: a.title}
```

That's good, but it doesn't help us if we were starting with our albums_by_miles query, and wanted to also select for Bobby Hutcherson. Ecto has a solution for us—the or_where keyword:

```
q = from [a,ar] in albums_by_miles, or_where: ar.name == "Bobby Hutcherson",
  select: %{artist: ar.name, album: a.title}
```

The or_where macro works exactly like where but it uses OR rather than AND when combined with other where clauses. If we add that to our query, we get this:

```
q = from [a,ar] in albums_by_miles, or_where: ar.name == "Bobby Hutcherson",
  select: %{artist: ar.name, album: a.title}
Repo.all(q)
#=> [%{album: "Kind Of Blue", artist: "Miles Davis"},
#=>  %{album: "Cookin' At The Plugged Nickel", artist: "Miles Davis"},
#=>  %{album: "Live At Montreaux", artist: "Bobby Hutcherson"}]
```

And when we run it, we get what we were looking for.

Other Ways to Use Queries

The Query module can be used for more than just reading data. We can use queries in some of the other *all functions we looked at in the last chapter. This allows us to perform update and delete operations on a specific collection of records. Let's take a look.

In the last chapter, we updated all the timestamps in the artists table with this code:

```
priv/examples/query_14.exs
Repo.update_all("artists", set: [updated_at: DateTime.utc_now])
```

In that example, we passed the table name as a String in the first parameter. But if you look at the documentation for update_all you'll see that this function does not expect a String but rather our new friend Ecto.Queryable. This means that you can also pass in a query, and be much more precise about which records are updated.

Let's say that we suspect there might be a misspelling in our tracks table. We can fix that by creating a query, then performing an update on the records that match that query:

```
q = from t in "tracks", where: t.title == "Autum Leaves"
Repo.update_all(q, set: [title: "Autumn Leaves"])
```

And if we want to be more Elixir-y, we could do it like this:

```
from(t in "tracks", where: t.title == "Autum Leaves")
|> Repo.update_all(set: [title: "Autumn Leaves"])
```

If we want to delete those records, we can use the same query with delete_all:

```
from(t in "tracks", where: t.title == "Autum Leaves")
|> Repo.delete_all
```

With queries in hand, we can now be very precise about our delete and update operations.

Wrapping Up

There's a lot more that can be said about queries. The Query API is rich and allows you to slice and dice your data in just about any way you can imagine. We've provided an introduction here, and a sense of how things go together, but we recommend you spend some time looking at the documentation to see all the things that you can do. In particular, look at the docs for the Ecto.Query module to see all the keywords available to you, and look at Ecto.Query.API to see all the utility functions that you can use within queries.

The Query module is powerful, but we did notice a couple of things early on that seemed tedious. First, it seems we always need to add a select clause. If we're using the same data types over and over, as most apps do, this could get old in a hurry. Also, having to type cast dynamic values in our queries seems like a lot of extra work. Fortunately for us, the Schema module can help us with both of these problems, so that will be the next stop on our tour. Read on to see how to make both these problems go away.

## CHAPTER 3

Connecting Your Tables to Elixir Structs with Schemas

Functional programs have a set of data structures that form the backbone of the codebase. In the music database we've been developing, we've got things like artists, albums, tracks, etc. The Ecto.Schema module helps us map those data structures to database tables, so we can seamlessly move data back and forth between our Elixir code and the database. You create the mappings with an elegant, concise DSL, then use *associations* to connect related structures together.

With schemas, you'll be able to create more streamlined operations for querying, inserting, and updating data. Schemas are quite flexible and can be used to map data from any data source (not just database tables) into our Elixir code. We'll explore some of those use cases later in the book.

We'll start by learning how to set up schemas, and look at the data types that Ecto supports. We'll then see how to integrate our schemas into queries, and convert some schema-less queries from the last chapter into leaner schema-based queries. We'll also look at some instances when it's best to avoid using schemas altogether.

From there, we'll look at how we can use associations to build relationships between database tables, and how to integrate those associations into queries. We'll wrap up by showing how schemas simplify inserting new records, even records with complicated associations.

Creating Schemas

Let's get our feet wet by looking at the DSL Ecto provides to create schemas. We'll use the DSL to specify the fields we want to map, and their data types.

Mapping Schema Fields

Let's start with our tracks table. We'll have just five fields for now:

- id: A unique ID for our track
- title: A string representing the track's title
- duration: The length of the track in seconds
- index: A number representing the track's position in an album
- number_of_plays: A counter that we increment every time we play the track

If you were writing an Elixir app that didn't use Ecto, you would most likely create a %Track{} struct to hold this data. You'd open a new file named track.ex and add something like this:

priv/examples/schema_01.exs
```
defmodule MusicDB.Track do
  defstruct [:id, :title, :duration, :index, :number_of_plays]
end
```

With Ecto, the process is similar. But rather than defstruct, we'll use the schema macro. Rather than a list of atoms, we'll provide fields. With these changes, our code will look like this:

```
defmodule MusicDB.Track do
  use Ecto.Schema

  schema "tracks" do
    field :title, :string
    field :duration, :integer
    field :index, :integer
    field :number_of_plays, :integer
    timestamps()
  end

end
```

This defines a new %Track{} struct, just like our last example did, but it goes further: it tells Ecto exactly how the fields in the struct connect to columns in the database.

This tiny block of code does more than you think, so we'll look at it bit by bit.

First, we've got a now-familiar use statement: use Ecto.Schema. We first saw this when discussing the Repo module. Just as we added use Ecto.Repo to our Repo, here we have use Ecto.Schema to make the functions from the Schema API available to this module.

Next, we call the Ecto.Schema.schema macro (which we can shorten to just schema, thanks to our use statement). This macro takes two arguments: the name of the table we want to map our schema to, and a block containing definitions for the fields we want to use.

Each field call specifies the name of the database column we want to use, and its datatype. Note that we don't have to specify every column—we only need to specify the columns that we plan to use in our Elixir code. If, for example, we decided that we don't want to use the number_of_plays column, we could simply remove that call to field. No harm, no foul.

Finally, we have timestamps. This macro adds two datetime fields to your schema, inserted_at and updated_at, representing times that the record was inserted into the database, and most recently changed, respectively. Ecto will update these values for you automatically on every insert and update operation. For this to work, however, you need to have inserted_at and updated_at columns in your database. When we start learning about database migrations in Chapter 6, Making Changes to Your Database, on page 101, we'll show you how to do this.

You may have noticed that we didn't include the id column. This is because by default, Ecto will create this field for you. It will be typed as an integer and assumed to be the primary key. This is typical for many databases but it's not universally consistent. If you are working with a database that has a different naming convention for primary keys, you need to be more explicit. For example, if the primary key of our tracks table was called track_id, we could specify that in our schema like this:

```
field :track_id, :id, primary_key: true
```

This uses the :id type to indicate that it is an integer-based primary key. We could also add the :autogenerate option to tell Ecto that the database will be generating this value for us.

The field function has a number of other options available that can alter the field definitions, and we'll look at a few of those later on. For a complete list, check Ecto's documentation.[1]

Working with Data Types

Ecto supports a number of different data types out of the box. The table on page 44, taken from the Schema docs,[2] shows the types you can use with the field call, and how they map to Elixir types.

---

1. https://hexdocs.pm/ecto/Ecto.Schema.html#field/3
2. https://hexdocs.pm/ecto/Ecto.Schema.html#content

Ecto Type	Elixir Type
:id	integer
:binary_id	binary
:integer	integer
:float	float
:boolean	boolean
:string	UTF-8 encoded string
:binary	binary
{:array, inner_type}	list
:map	map
{:map, inner_type}	map
:decimal	Decimal
:date	Date
:time	Time
:naive_datetime	NaiveDateTime
:utc_datetime	DateTime

The :naive_datetime type is a datetime value that has no associated time zone information. If you use utc_datetime the value must be a DateTime struct with its time zone set to UTC. Ecto will raise an error if you attempt to use a value with a different time zone.

The time, naive_datetime, and utc_datetime types used to store microsecond information in the columns that use them, but this is no longer the case. If you do need microsecond precision, you should use one of the corresponding types: time_usec, naive_datetime_usec, or utc_datetime_usec.

The :map type allows you to store Elixir maps into the database. The storage strategy differs depending on the database. In MySQL, maps are stored as text fields, but Postgres has first-class support for maps via its jsonb type and these fields are actually queryable. As of this writing, the Ecto team strongly recommends that your maps use string keys, rather than atoms. In some cases, storing a map with atom keys will work correctly but when retrieving, Ecto will always return maps with string keys.

If you need a type that is not currently supported, it's possible to create your own custom type using an API provided by Ecto. We'll look at some examples of this when we get to Chapter 10, Creating and Using Custom Types, on page 145. You can also read the documentation for Ecto.Type.[3]

---

3. https://hexdocs.pm/ecto/Ecto.Type.html

Writing Queries with Schemas

When we looked at queries in the last chapter, we deliberately chose to write them without schemas. This is still a good choice in some circumstances, but schemas provide some helpful shortcuts and we promised that we'd revisit them later. Now's the time. In this section, we'll start writing queries that work with schemas, and we'll also consider when it's best not to.

Converting a Schema-less Query

Let's look at a query we ran in the last chapter:

```
priv/examples/schema_02.exs
artist_id = "1"
q = from "artists", where: [id: type(^artist_id, :integer)],
  select: [:name]
Repo.all(q)
#=> [%{name: "Miles Davis"}]
```

As you may recall, artist_id is initialized as a string, but the id column in the artists table is an integer, so we have to convert the value ourselves using the type function.

In addition, we have to use the select option to specify what columns we want returned to us. This is not so bad since we're only fetching one value, but consider what this would look like with the tracks table:

```
track_id = "1"
q = from "tracks", where: [id: type(^track_id, :integer)],
  select: [:title, :duration, :index, :number_of_plays]
```

Specifying all those fields every time could get tedious quickly.

Schemas can help us with both of these issues. Using our new %Track{} schema, we can rewrite the query like this:

```
alias MusicDB.Track

track_id = "1"
q = from Track, where: [id: ^track_id]
```

Notice that we've replaced the string "tracks" with the name of the schema module we created earlier. This tells Ecto that our query is referencing a schema, rather than the name of a database table. Adding the alias in the first line lets us use the module name without its full namespace—most Ecto developers follow this convention.

Integrating the schema into the query does several things for us. First, *it performs the type conversion of track_id automatically.* Remember that Ecto added the id field to our schema, and typed it as an integer. Having the type specified in the schema allows Ecto to do any needed conversions on our behalf (within reason, of course).

Second, *we can remove the select: option*—Ecto will fetch all of the fields defined in our schema, unless told otherwise.

Finally, *the return value is a schema struct.* Instead of getting back a list or a map, we get a %Track{} struct, populated with the values from the corresponding database record:

```
track_id = "1"
q = from Track, where: [id: ^track_id]
Repo.all(q)
#=> [%MusicDB.Track{__meta__: #Ecto.Schema.Metadata<:loaded, "tracks">,
#=> album: #Ecto.Association.NotLoaded<association :album is not loaded>,
#=> album_id: 1, duration: 544, id: 1, index: 1,
#=> inserted_at: ~N[2017-03-13 13:25:38], number_of_plays: 0,
#=> title: "So What", updated_at: ~N[2017-03-13 13:25:38]}]
```

The select option is still available to us, if we want it. We'll still get a %Track{} struct back, but any fields we didn't specify in the select will be set to nil:

```
q = from Track, where: [id: ^track_id], select: [:title]
Repo.all(q)
#=> [%MusicDB.Track{__meta__: #Ecto.Schema.Metadata<:loaded, "tracks">,
#=>   album: #Ecto.Association.NotLoaded<association :album is not loaded>,
#=>   album_id: nil, duration: nil, id: nil, index: nil, inserted_at: nil,
#=>   number_of_plays: nil, title: "So What", updated_at: nil}]
```

Query bindings work exactly like they did when we were working without schemas. We can add one to the current query to help clean up our where clause:

```
q = from t in Track, where: t.id == ^track_id
```

Query bindings aren't necessary for a small query like this, but developers seem to use them most of the time, so this style of query is what you'll most likely see out in the wild.

When Not to Use Schemas

We introduced schemas late in the game to drive home an important point: you don't have to use them. As we saw in the last chapter, we were able to query for just about anything we needed without them. But they come in handy when working directly with the core data structures of your application.

Our %Track{} struct is a great example. We know we'll be using that set of fields throughout our code. Defining it in one place and letting Ecto handle the select statements and the data type conversion for us makes a lot of sense.

But for other types of queries, using schemas doesn't buy you much. This is especially true for queries used in reports, where we often need fields from many different tables, combined with aggregate functions like count and avg. These don't return data in shapes we're likely to re-use.

Let's say we wanted to get a list of all of the artists in our database and the number of albums associated with each one. We could use the Artist or Album schemas to help us write the query, but they wouldn't help much. The return value we want doesn't really look like the shape of either of those schemas, and we're not concerned about casting any inputs to specific types. All we really want is a list of maps, where each map has the artist's name and the number of albums. In this case, writing a query without a schema is a good choice:

```
priv/examples/schema_03.exs
q = from a in "artists",
  join: al in "albums",
  on: a.id == al.artist_id,
  group_by: a.name,
  select: %{artist: a.name, number_of_albums: count(al.id)}
Repo.all(q)
#=> [%{artist: "Miles Davis", number_of_albums: 2},
#=> %{artist: "Bobby Hutcherson", number_of_albums: 1},
#=> %{artist: "Bill Evans", number_of_albums: 2}]
```

By skipping schemas and crafting a custom select, we can have Ecto return the data we need in exactly the shape that we want. Schemas should make things easier, not harder; so if you're writing a query and the schemas seem to be getting in your way, consider rewriting the query without them.

Inserting and Deleting with Schemas

When we first looked at the Repo module in Chapter 1, Getting Started with Repo, on page 3, we looked at the insert_all and delete_all functions for inserting and deleting data. Ecto provides these functions so you can perform these operations without schemas (which, as we saw in the last section, is sometimes the best approach). When you are working with schemas, Repo has two parallel functions, insert and delete. Let's take a look at those now. But before we start, let's run mix ecto.reset once again to get our data back into a clean state.

Inserting with Schemas

Here's a snippet we ran earlier to insert an artists record for John Coltrane using insert_all:

```
priv/examples/schema_04.exs
Repo.insert_all("artists", [[name: "John Coltrane"]])
#=> {1, nil}
```

Here's how we could do the same thing using Repo.insert and our Artist schema:

```
Repo.insert(%Artist{name: "John Coltrane"})
#=> {:ok, %MusicDB.Artist{__meta__: #Ecto.Schema.Metadata<:loaded, "artists">,
#=>  id: 4, name: "John Coltrane", ...}
```

Notice the return value of the two functions is quite different. When we used insert_all we got back the number of records affected by the operation (just one, in this case) and any values we requested using the returning option—we didn't supply that option in this example, so we got nil.

When we instead used insert, we got :ok, indicating that the operation succeeded, and a new Artist struct representing the record we just inserted. The returned struct represents the record *after* the insertion completed, so we can see the new id value assigned by the database.

It's also possible to mix the two approaches by calling insert_all with a schema rather than a table name:

```
Repo.insert_all(Artist, [[name: "John Coltrane"]])
#=> {1, nil}
```

Which function you choose can vary depending on your needs. One limitation of insert is that you're limited to inserting a single record at a time, whereas insert_all can handle multiple records at once. But if you're using schemas and you just need to insert one record, insert might be more convenient. You should also consider what return value you prefer: if it's important to get a fully populated struct back, you'll want to use insert.

Deleting with Schemas

Now let's look at deleting records. When we first looked at delete_all in Chapter 1, Getting Started with Repo, on page 3 we used it to remove all of the records in the table:

```
priv/examples/schema_05.exs
Repo.delete_all("tracks")
```

When we learned about queries, we were able to delete records with more precision—here we're deleting all the records that have a misspelled title:

```
from(t in "tracks", where: t.title == "Autum Leaves")
|> Repo.delete_all
```

We use Repo.delete when we have a single schema struct and want to delete its corresponding record from the database. Just like insert, it can only handle one record at a time:

```
track = Repo.get_by(Track, title: "The Moontrane")
Repo.delete(track)
#=> {:ok, %MusicDB.Track{__meta__: #Ecto.Schema.Metadata<:deleted, "tracks">,
#=>   id: 28, title: "The Moontrane", ...}
```

The operation succeeded so we got :ok along with a struct representing the record we just deleted. At this point, however, the record no longer exists in the database.

Having now learned about how to insert and delete with schemas, you might be curious about updates. There is indeed an update function available in Repo, but it uses *changesets* rather than schema structs to perform updates.

Changesets are a critical component in Ecto's approach to making changes to the database. In fact, the insert and delete functions we just looked at return changesets if the operations fail. We'll be looking at changesets in detail in Chapter 4, Making Changes with Changesets, on page 63, and we'll see some examples of updates then.

Adding Associations to Schemas

Databases are about tables, *and the relationships between them.* Consider the data model we've been working with throughout this book. Artists have many albums, and albums have many tracks as well as many genres. Let's drill down to one specific relationship first, the one between artists and albums.

These two data types reside in separate tables, but they're closely related: each of the albums belongs to a particular artist. At the database level, we connect the two tables with a *foreign key:* in this case, the artist_id column in albums refers to the primary key of the artists table. In Ecto, we use *associations* to model these relationships. Associations help reflect the connections between database tables in our Elixir code.

In this section, we'll look at the different types of associations that Ecto supports, and how we can add them to our schemas. We'll then look at how to modify our queries to work with associations, and how they can help us insert new records with ease.

One-to-Many and One-to-One Associations

To get our first taste of associations, let's create a schema for our albums table. Based on what we learned in the last section, we know that it will start with something like this:

```
priv/examples/schema_06.exs
defmodule MusicDB.Album do
  use Ecto.Schema

  schema "albums" do
    field :title, :string
    field :release_date, :date
  end

end
```

This is a good start: we have title as a string, and release_date as a date. But we know that albums have tracks, and we want to create an association between this schema and the %Track{} schema we created earlier.

Albums have a one-to-many relationship to tracks; that is, one album will have many tracks, but a given track will belong to only one album (we will for now ignore the complexity of modeling compilation albums). We can express this relationship in our schema with the has_many function:

```
defmodule MusicDB.Album do
  use Ecto.Schema

  schema "albums" do
    field :title, :string
    field :release_date, :date

    has_many :tracks, MusicDB.Track
  end

end
```

This call states that our %Album{} schema will have a field called tracks, which will consist of zero or more instances of the %Track{} struct. In this association, the %Album{} record is called the *parent record* and the %Track{} records are the *child records*.

For this to work, Ecto will be looking for a column named album_id in the tracks table to connect the tracks to the albums. We built these tables following Ecto's conventions, but if you're working with a legacy database that uses a different naming scheme, you can still make the association work by specifying the foreign key explicitly.

For example, if the tracks table used album_number rather than album_id for the foreign key, we could create the association like this:

```
has_many :tracks, MusicDB.Track, foreign_key: :album_number
```

This tells Ecto that it should look for a column named album_number in the tracks table to find the foreign key that points back to the albums table.

In addition to has_many, Ecto also provides the has_one association. This works exactly like has_many but it limits the number of associated records to zero or one. This association is used much less often than has_many, but it can be useful in some cases.

Belongs-to Associations

Most of the time, you'll want your associations to work in both directions. Just as you want to refer to tracks from an album record, you'll often want to refer to an album from a track. We can use the belongs_to association as the reverse of has_many and has_one. Let's create the association from tracks back to albums. We can do that by adding a belongs_to call in the %Track{} schema:

priv/examples/schema_07.exs
```
schema "tracks" do
  field :title, :string
  # other fields here...

  belongs_to :album, MusicDB.Album
end
```

This establishes the association from a track back to its album. As before, Ecto will assume that the tracks table will have a field named album_id that provides the foreign key, but if the field has a different name, we can use the foreign_key: option to specify it.

Now we have a has_many association between albums and tracks, as well as its inverse belongs_to association. But albums have another association as well. They are the child in a one-to-many relationship with artists. We can set that up by adding a belongs_to call to the %Album{} schema, and a has_many call to %Artist{}:

```
# in album.ex
schema "albums" do
  # field definitions here...

  has_many :tracks, MusicDB.Track
  belongs_to :artist, MusicDB.Artist
end

# in artist.ex
schema "artists" do
  # field definitions here...

  has_many :albums, MusicDB.Album
end
```

The %Album{} schema now has associations in two directions: it has_many tracks, and it belongs_to artist.

> ### Which schema gets has_many and which gets belongs_to?
>
> When working with one-to-many or one-to-one relationships, belongs_to goes on the schema with the foreign key. For example, tracks has the foreign key album_id which is the basis of the association, so it gets the belongs_to call, and albums gets has_many. By the same token, albums has the foreign key artist_id, so it gets a belongs_to call for %Artist{} and %Artist{} gets a has_many for albums.

Nested Associations

In the last section, we added a has_many association from artist to albums, and another has_many association from albums to tracks. The relationships between the tables look something like this:

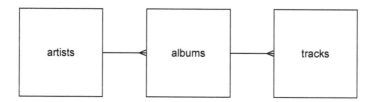

As we look at the model, it's easy to imagine cases where you might want to refer to tracks directly from an artist record, without having to go through the albums. This is called a *nested association*, and we can create one using a variation of has_many or has_one.

To create this association, we'll add another has_many call to the %Artist{} schema, but this time we'll add the through: option to spell out the path between %Artist{} and %Track{}:

priv/examples/schema_08.exs
```
schema "artists" do
  # field definitions here...

  has_many :albums, MusicDB.Album
  has_many :tracks, through: [:albums, :tracks]
end
```

The through: option takes a list representing the steps to get from the current schema to the schema we want to associate with. The first item is albums, which is the association we created on the previous line. Ecto will look in that schema to find the next item, tracks. This nesting can go as deep as you need it to, but be judicious: more than two or three levels is likely to get messy.

With this in place, we can refer to an artist's %Track{} records directly from the %Artist{} record without having to go through the albums.

Note that belongs_to is not supported for nested associations. You can't, for example, create an association from %Track{} back up to %Artist{}. You would have to go explicitly through each step in your code: track.album.artist.

Many-to-Many Associations

We're now going to look at a more complex association: many-to-many. These relationships are not as straightforward as belongs-to relationships because you need an extra table to implement them.

A good example of a many-to-many relationship is assigning genres to albums. Genres describe the musical style of an album, for example jazz, classical, rock, blues, death polka, and so on. We want to be able to assign more than one genre for each album. But we also want to associate each genre with more than one album. For example, we will have one record in the genres table for "jazz," and we want to associate that record with many different albums.

The traditional way to model this relationship is to create an extra table that maps the relationships between the two other tables. This is called a *join table*, and usually looks something like this:

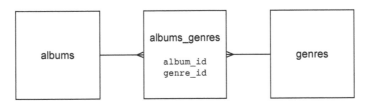

Here, the albums_genres table exists solely to hold the associations between albums and genres. It creates the link between the album record and the genre record by holding two foreign keys, one for each table. This allows an album to be associated with any number of genres, and a genre can be associated with any number of albums. We can sever an association between an album and a genre by deleting a record from this table.

Ecto has excellent support for many-to-many associations. Setting up the association is similar to setting up a has_many through: association. The critical component is the join_through option, which tells Ecto where to find the join table. Assuming the table structure shown in the previous diagram, we would use the following code to create the association:

priv/examples/schema_09.exs
```
# in album.ex
schema "albums" do
  # field definitions here...

  many_to_many :genres, MusicDB.Genre, join_through: MusicDB.AlbumGenre
end

# in genre.ex
schema "genres" do
  # field definitions here...

  many_to_many :albums, MusicDB.Album, join_through: MusicDB.AlbumGenre
end

# in album_genre.ex
schema "albums_genres" do
  # field definitions here...

  belongs_to :albums, MusicDB.Album
  belongs_to :genres, MusicDB.Genre
end
```

Once this is set up, albums and genres can refer to each other without going through the albums_genres schema.

This is fairly concise, but it's possible to tighten it up even further. If we're only going have to have album_id and genre_id fields in the albums_genres table, we don't need to create a schema for that table to make the many-to-many association work. We just need to create the table, then refer to the table name in the join_through option, like so:

```
# in album.ex
schema "albums" do
  # field definitions here...

  many_to_many :genres, MusicDB.Genre, join_through: "albums_genres"
end

# in genre.ex
schema "genres" do
  # field definitions here...

  many_to_many :albums, MusicDB.Album, join_through: "albums_genres"
end
```

If you want to use any other fields besides the foreign keys in your join table (timestamps, for example, or other metadata), this simplified version won't work: you'll need to create a schema like we did in the previous example and map the fields you're interested in. But if all you need are the foreign keys, you can skip the extra schema and let Ecto figure it out for you.

Ecto's support for many-to-many associations makes modeling this type of relationship straightforward, and gets a lot of the tedious boilerplate out of your way. many_to_many can also be used for *polymorphic associations*—we'll be taking a closer look at that technique in Chapter 14, Creating Polymorphic Associations, on page 179.

Working with Associations in Queries

Now that we've got some associations defined, let's put them to work. Go to the music_db project and open up a mix session with iex -S mix.

First grab the record for the album *Kind Of Blue:*

priv/examples/schema_10.exs
```
album = Repo.get_by(Album, title: "Kind Of Blue")
```

Our gut tells us that if we want to see the tracks for this album, we would just do this:

```
album.tracks
```

But our gut is wrong. Instead, we get this:

```
#Ecto.Association.NotLoaded<association :tracks is not loaded>
```

This is not an error. It's a placeholder value indicating that the tracks records associated with this album have not yet been retrieved from the database.

You might well wonder why Ecto doesn't just load the records for you when you ask for them, and in fact some database libraries do—it's a feature called *lazy loading*. With lazy loading, the library checks to see if the associated records have been loaded when you try to refer to them. If not, it fetches them from the database automatically and makes them available to you.

In some ways, that seems like the right thing to do. We have an album record and we want the associated tracks, so it makes sense that the library would make things easy for us and go fetch the tracks when we ask for them. The trouble is that it can lead to performance problems as the database grows. Consider the following pseudocode:

```
albums = get_album_records_from_database()
for album in albums do
  print album.title
  for tracks in album.tracks do # tracks are lazy loaded here
    print "  * #{track.title} "
  end
end
```

Assume for a moment that this code actually worked. Because of lazy loading, each time we pass through the loop over the albums, that innocent-looking call to album.tracks would trigger a database query to fetch the tracks associated with the album. That's not a big deal if you only have a few album records in your database. But imagine if you had 5000 albums. That block of code would trigger 5001 SQL queries: one to fetch the albums, then 5000 more to get the tracks for each of the albums.

This is the infamous *N+1 Query problem*, so called because you need one query to fetch the parent records, then N more queries to fetch the child records (where N is the number of parent records).

It's caused no small amount of weeping and gnashing of teeth among developers trying to solve application performance problems. It's especially pernicious because it sneaks up on you. The app runs fine at first, but over time, it starts to slow down as the database gets larger and larger. There's nothing in the code that explicitly indicates database queries are being run. It's happening behind the scenes, and unless you have a clear understanding of how lazy loading works and know exactly what you're looking for, this kind of problem can be easy to miss.

Ecto's solution to this problem is straightforward: it doesn't support lazy loading. You have to be specific about what you want and when you want it. This involves a little more typing, but it prevents N+1 problems from popping up in the far-flung future, and it makes the code very clear about when Ecto is communicating with the database. Anyone looking at your code later on will appreciate that clarity (especially if that person is you).

Ecto provides a few options for loading associated records. The first is to add the preload option in your query for the parent records:

```
albums = Repo.all(from a in Album, preload: :tracks)
```

If you've already loaded the parent records and want to fetch the associations after the fact, you can use the Repo.preload function:

```
albums =
  Album
  |> Repo.all
  |> Repo.preload(:tracks)
```

In both of these cases, you end up with all of the album records, with each album having its associated tracks. And in both cases, only two database queries are executed: one to fetch all the albums, and another to fetch all the tracks. Regardless of the size of the albums table, you can be sure that only two queries will be run.

The preload statements can handle nested associations using keyword list syntax ([]). If you were grabbing records from the artists table, and you wanted to get the associated albums and their tracks, you could do this:

```
Repo.all(from a in Artist, preload: [albums: :tracks])
```

In this case, you would get a rather large dataset: Ecto would return all of the artists, with all of their associated albums, and all of the tracks associated with those albums.

If you want to grab parent records and child records together in one query, you can use preload in combination with join. This query will get albums and associated track records together, but it will limit the results to only the albums with a track titled "Freddie Freeloader":

```
q = from a in Album,
  join: t in assoc(a, :tracks),
  where: t.title == "Freddie Freeloader",
  preload: [tracks: t]
```

Here we use the Ecto.assoc/2 function to specify that we want to join on the :tracks association we defined in our Album schema. By adding the reference to the query binding t in the preload option, we're telling Ecto to load the album and track records in the same query.

This approach reduces the number of queries sent to the database, but it can increase the amount of data that's sent back. We'll talk some more about this trade-off in Chapter 17, Tuning for Performance, on page 201.

Optimizing Associations with Embedded Schemas

Ecto's protection against N+1 queries helps prevent runaway situations where our code is making huge numbers of queries for what appears to be a simple operation. But even then, fetching associated records always requires an extra round-trip to the database, and there may be situations where you want to avoid it. You might be working with associated records that always need to be loaded along with the parents, or you may be in a performance-critical situation where you need to eke out every last ounce of speed that you can. In cases like these, Ecto provides *embedded schemas*.

With embedded schemas, associated records are stored in a single database column along with the rest of the parent record's values. When you load the parent record, the child records come right along with it. The implementation of this feature varies between databases. With PostgreSQL, Ecto uses the jsonb column type to store the records as an array of key/value pairs. For MySQL, Ecto converts the records into a JSON string and stores them as text. The end result, however, is the same: the embedded records are loaded into the appropriate Elixir structs and are available in a single query without having to call preload.

Embedded schemas require a particular setup in the database, and some key differences in behavior exist compared with the associations we've seen so far. For these reasons, we've created a separate chapter to cover this topic, Chapter 13, Working with Embedded Schemas, on page 171). This chapter will go into the entire life cycle of working with embeds: database setup, inserting, updating, and so on. For now, just bear in mind that you have more than one option when modeling associations, and, depending on your needs, embedded schemas might be a better approach.

Deleting Records with Associations

An important thing to consider with associations is what should happen to child records when a parent record is deleted. For example, if we delete an album, what should we do with the associated tracks? Ecto provides the on_delete: option to specify the desired behavior, but the exact implementation will vary depending on the database you're using. Let's take a closer look.

One approach is to define the behavior when creating the association. The has_many, has_one, and many_to_many functions all support the on_delete: option, which can have one of three values:

- :nothing—This is the default behavior: Ecto won't try to do anything to the child records if the parent is deleted.

- :nilify_all—Ecto updates all of the child records, setting the foreign key referring to the parent record to null. At that point, the child records are no longer associated with any parent record.

- :delete_all—Ecto deletes all of the child records along with the parent record.

There's a catch to this, however. Many databases, including Postgres, allow you to specify this behavior in the database itself when you first create the table. In those databases, the work of deleting or nilifying the child records is handled by the database, rather than by Ecto. If that's how your database works, setting a value for :on_delete in the schema definition will have no effect.

You'll need to check the database you're using and find if it supports this feature; if so, you'll need to use on_delete in the database migration rather than when declaring the association (we'll be looking at migrations in detail in Chapter 6, Making Changes to Your Database, on page 101).

In either case, if you set the value to :nothing, deleting a parent record with child records will most likely fail. This behavior also varies among databases, but most have *foreign key integrity constraints*, meaning that the database will prevent you from deleting any records that other records refer to.

If you want to delete the parent record, you must manually run the same steps as nilify_all or delete_all: either update the child records so that they no longer refer to the parent, or delete them. With this approach, you'll want to be sure that all of these steps succeed together. We'll look at ways to do that in Chapter 5, Making Multiple Changes with Transactions and Multi, on page 87, but in this case, you're probably better off using delete_all and letting the database handle it. The operation will be more performant and reliable if it doesn't require additional database calls.

Using Schemas to Seed a Database

Once you've set up schemas for your tables, inserting new records, even records with nested associations, can be done very concisely.

Recall how we inserted a new artists record using Repo.insert_all:

priv/examples/schema_11.exs
```
Repo.insert_all("artists", [[name: "John Coltrane"]])
#=> {1, nil}
```

With insert_all, we had to provide the table name, and a list of fields containing the new record's values. And if we wanted the ID of the new record, we had to ask for it with the returning option (which is only available with Postgres):

```
Repo.insert_all("artists", [[name: "John Coltrane"]], returning: [:id])
#=> {1, [%{id: 8}]}
```

As we saw earlier, with schemas, we can use the Repo.insert function and pass it a struct representing the record we want to insert:

```
Repo.insert(%Artist{name: "John Coltrane"})
```

The return value is a two-element tuple. The first element will either be :ok or :error, indicating whether or not the insertion was successful. If it's :ok, the second element will be the newly inserted record:

```
{:ok, artist} = Repo.insert(%Artist{name: "John Coltrane"})
#=> %MusicDB.Artist{__meta__: #Ecto.Schema.Metadata<:loaded, "artists">,
#=> albums: #Ecto.Association.NotLoaded<association :albums is not loaded>,
#=> id: 8, inserted_at: ~N[2017-07-14 06:35:05],
#=> name: "John Coltrane",
#=> tracks: #Ecto.Association.NotLoaded<association :tracks is not loaded>,
#=> updated_at: ~N[2017-07-14 06:35:05]}
```

Note that the id field has been correctly populated with the autogenerated
primary key value.

If the first element is :error, the second element will be a Changeset representing the values we tried to insert. We'll be talking about changesets in
depth in the next chapter.

Now consider creating a new Album record for this artist. You might think that
you'd have to insert the artist record first, get the id of the new record, then
create the album record with artist_id set to the id of the new artist. But thanks
to the association between our Artist and Album schema, we can insert the two
records at the same time:

```
Repo.insert(
  %Artist{
    name: "John Coltrane",
    albums: [
      %Album{
        title: "A Love Supreme"
      }
    ]
  }
)
```

Even deeply nested associations can be inserted in this way, and you can
insert multiple associations at once. Here we'll create an artist record for John
Coltrane, an album, the tracks for the album, and the album's genre, all in
one call to insert:

```
Repo.insert(
  %Artist{
    name: "John Coltrane",
    albums: [
      %Album{
        title: "A Love Supreme",
        tracks: [
          %Track{title: "Part 1: Acknowledgement", index: 1},
          %Track{title: "Part 2: Resolution", index: 2},
          %Track{title: "Part 3: Pursuance", index: 3},
          %Track{title: "Part 4: Psalm", index: 4},
        ],
```

```
      genres: [
        %Genre{name: "spiritual jazz"},
      ]
    }
  ]
 }
)
```

This is extremely handy for database setup scripts or other situations where you need to create a lot of database records at once. If you look at the priv/repo/seeds.exs in the music_db project, you can see how we used this technique to populate all of the sample data with just a few insert statements.

Wrapping Up

In this chapter, we learned how schemas allow us to create data structures that we can map to our database tables. This is how you'll be using schemas most of the time, but schemas are actually very flexible and can be used in a number of different ways. We'll be looking at some examples later on in the book.

At the end of the chapter, we saw how schemas make it easy for us to insert lots of records at once, even records with complex nested associations. There's one issue that we glossed over, however: making sure that the data we're inserting is valid, and catching any errors that might arise. This is a critical part of maintaining the integrity of our data, and the Changeset module is here to help, so we'll look at that next.

## CHAPTER 4

Making Changes with Changesets

At the end of the last chapter, we saw how schemas provide a quick method for inserting new records into the database, even with associated records. But a database is only as good as the quality of the data that it contains, so we need to be careful about the modifications we make to that data. The Ecto.Changeset module provides a rich data structure and a wide array of functions that helps us manage making changes safely and securely.

In this chapter, we will take a deep dive into the world of changesets. We will start by taking a high-level look at the process of making a change, then look at each step of the process in detail: casting and filtering user-provided data, validating the data, and capturing errors. Finally, we will look at how changesets help us with the often-tricky process of working with associations and embeds.

Introducing Changesets

Changesets manage the update process by breaking it into three distinct stages: casting and filtering user input, validating the input, then sending the input to the database and capturing the result. If you think of it as a pipeline, it would look something like this:

```
data
|> cast_and_filter_fields
|> validate_change
|> validate_another_change
|> send_to_database
```

We'll look at each step in detail, but here's what the process looks like in code. The following example inserts a new Artist record, based on data supplied by the user:

```
priv/examples/changeset_01.exs
import Ecto.Changeset

params = %{name: "Gene Harris"}
changeset =
  %Artist{}
  |> cast(params, [:name])
  |> validate_required([:name])

case Repo.insert(changeset) do
  {:ok, artist} -> IO.puts("Record for #{artist.name} was created.")
  {:error, changeset} -> IO.inspect(changeset.errors)
end
```

As this example demonstrates, changesets help us with the entire life cycle of making a change, starting with raw data, and ending with the operation succeeding or failing at the database level. Let's now zoom in on each step.

Casting and Filtering

The first step is to take the raw input data that you want to apply to the database and generate an Ecto.Changeset struct. We call this "casting and filtering" because we perform any needed type casting operations (for example, turning a string into an integer), and we filter out any values we don't want to use. You can do this two different ways, depending on where your data is coming from. We'll look at both in the following sections.

Creating Changesets Using Internal Data

If the data is internal to the application (that is, you're generating the data yourself in your application code), you can create a changeset using the Ecto.Changeset.change function. Here's how you would create a changeset that inserts a new Artist record:

```
priv/examples/changeset_02.exs
import Ecto.Changeset

changeset = change(%Artist{name: "Charlie Parker"})
```

The import statement makes all of the functions in Ecto.Changeset available to our code. For brevity, we won't include this in the rest of the examples.

To make changes to an existing record, the process is similar, but instead of passing in a new struct, we use a record fetched from Repo:

```
artist = Repo.get_by(Artist, name: "Bobby Hutcherson")
changeset = change(artist)
```

We can add the data we'd like to change as optional arguments to the change function. This is how we might change the name field to something more formal:

```
artist = Repo.get_by(Artist, name: "Bobby Hutcherson")
changeset = change(artist, name: "Robert Hutcherson")
```

At this point, changeset is just a data structure in memory—no communication with the database has happened yet. As we've seen with the Repository pattern, nothing happens with the database until we get Repo involved. If we wanted to commit the change, we'd need to call Repo.update(changeset) and check the result to see if it succeeded.

Before we do that, we can take a peek at the changes that will be applied. The changes field of our changeset tells us what's going to be updated:

```
changeset.changes
#=> %{name: "Robert Hutcherson"}
```

We can also use the change function to add more changes to a changeset that's already been created—instead of passing in an Artist struct as the first argument, we can pass another changeset. Using the changeset value we created in the last code example, we could add the artist's birth date to the list of items we're going to update:

```
changeset = change(changeset, birth_date: ~D[1941-01-27])
```

And of course, it's possible to add both changes into a single change call:

```
artist = Repo.get_by(Artist, name: "Bobby Hutcherson")
changeset = change(artist, name: "Robert Hutcherson",
  birth_date: ~D[1941-01-27])
```

In either case, calling changes will now show both of the values that we are updating:

```
changeset.changes
#=> %{birth_date: ~D[1941-01-27], name: "Robert Hutcherson"}
```

The data we've been using so far has been generated in our code. In most cases however, the data you want to apply will be coming from outside of the controlled environment of your own code: forms your application presents to end users, API calls, command-line parameters, CSVs or other data files, and so forth. To deal with this potentially unruly data, Ecto provides the cast function for creating changesets.

Creating Changesets Using External Data

When working with data coming from external sources, it's important to take extra care. The cast function plays a similar role to change, as it's used to take raw data and return a Changeset struct, but it's got a few extra features to help make sure you're getting only the data you want.

The cast function has three required arguments. The first is the same as change: it should be a data structure representing the record you want to apply your changes to. This could be a new schema struct (for example %Artist{}), a schema struct representing a record fetched from the database, or another changeset.

The second argument is a map containing raw data that you want to apply. The third is a list of the parameters that you'll allow to be added to the changeset. It acts like a filter: only parameters specified in the list will be added to the changeset. The rest will be discarded.

Here is how we could create a changeset for a new Artist record using user-supplied parameters. (In the following examples, we'll use the params variable to represent values supplied by the user.)

```
priv/examples/changeset_03.exs
# values provided by the user
params = %{"name" => "Charlie Parker", "birth_date" => "1920-08-29",
  "instrument" => "alto sax"}

changeset = cast(%Artist{}, params, [:name, :birth_date])
changeset.changes
#=> %{birth_date: ~D[1920-08-29], name: "Charlie Parker"}
```

Take a close look at the result of the changes call, and you'll see what cast has done for us. First, the instrument value provided in the params map does not appear in the changeset. This is because we only specified :name and :birth_date in the list of allowed values, so Ecto dropped the instrument field for us. This can be useful when importing data from sources you don't control. If you were importing data from a CSV, for example, there could be extra columns of data that you don't need. This setting helps you get rid of them.

Second, the call to cast converted the birth_date value from the string "1920-08-29" to an Elixir Date struct. As the name suggests, cast will perform type casting when turning the raw input into a changeset, whenever it can. In this case, our Artist schema defined birth_date as the :date type, so Ecto parsed the string value into a Date when creating the changeset. This worked because we received the date in a standard format. If we got an unknown date format, Ecto would not be able to cast it and the changeset would be invalid. We'll talk more about validating changesets in the next section.

By default, the cast function will treat the empty string "" as nil when creating the changeset. But there may be times when you want other values turned into nil as well. For example, when working with spreadsheets, you'll often see data that looks like this:

```
params = %{"name" => "Charlie Parker", "birth_date" => "NULL"}
```

Instead of getting an empty cell, you get the string "NULL." We can tell Ecto that we want to consider "NULL" an empty value, by adding the empty_values option to cast:

```
params = %{"name" => "Charlie Parker", "birth_date" => "NULL"}
changeset = cast(%Artist{}, params, [:name, :birth_date],
  empty_values: ["", "NULL"])
changeset.changes
#=> %{name: "Charlie Parker"}
```

By adding "NULL" to the empty_values option, we were able to treat the birth_date value as empty, and Ecto dropped it from the list of changes. You can specify as many different values as you need, but don't forget to include "" if you want to convert empty strings as well.

Validating Your Data

We've completed the first step of making a change to the database, and we have a Changeset struct with the changes we want to apply. But before we send it off to the database, we want to make sure that the data we've got is correct. Ecto provides two tools to help us check the integrity of our data: *validations* and *constraints*. They perform similar functions, but differ in the way that they're implemented. We'll explore each of them in the rest of this section.

Working with Validations

Validations are utility functions provided by the Ecto.Changeset module to help check the integrity of your data. If you look at the module documentation, the validation functions are easy to spot because they all start with validate_: validate_required, validate_format, validate_number, and the like. They all take a changeset as the first parameter, and they all return a new changeset with the validation applied. This arrangement lends itself very nicely to working with the pipe operator:

```
priv/examples/changeset_04.exs
params = %{"name" => "Thelonius Monk", "birth_date" => "1917-10-10"}
changeset =
  %Artist{}
  |> cast(params, [:name, :birth_date])
  |> validate_required([:name, :birth_date])
  |> validate_length(:name, min: 3)
```

In this example, we have two validations. validate_required checks that we have non-empty values for name and birth_date, and validate_length will make sure that the name value is at least three characters.

Validations are run immediately when called, and the returned changeset will reflect the result of the validation. If the validation succeeds, the valid? field on the changeset will be true; if not, valid? will be false, and we can look at the errors field to see what the problem is.

Let's try this out by removing the required birth_date field from the params:

```
params = %{"name" => "Thelonius Monk"}
changeset =
  %Artist{}
  |> cast(params, [:name, :birth_date])
  |> validate_required([:name, :birth_date])
  |> validate_length(:name, min: 3)

changeset.valid?
#=> false
changeset.errors
#=> [birth_date: {"can't be blank", [validation: :required]}]
```

If one validation fails, Ecto will still run the others, and the errors field will show all of the errors grouped together:

```
params = %{"name" => "x"}
changeset =
  %Artist{}
  |> cast(params, [:name, :birth_date])
  |> validate_required([:name, :birth_date])
  |> validate_length(:name, min: 3)

changeset.errors
#=> [name: {"should be at least %{count} character(s)",
#=> [count: 3, validation: :length, min: 3]},
#=> birth_date: {"can't be blank", [validation: :required]}]
```

This output, while rich in details, is perhaps not the easiest to work with, particularly if you have several errors. The Ecto.Changeset.traverse_errors function can help: it lets you iterate through each of the errors and transform it into any form you like.

The documentation provides the following example that turns the errors into a map, where the keys are the fields that have errors, and the values are lists of errors for each of those fields:

```
traverse_errors(changeset, fn {msg, opts} ->
  Enum.reduce(opts, msg, fn {key, value}, acc ->
    String.replace(acc, "%{#{key}}", to_string(value))
  end)
end)
#=> %{birth_date: ["can't be blank"],
#=> name: ["should be at least 3 character(s)"]}
```

With that map, you could attach error messages to form fields in your UI, or just create a list of strings showing all the errors at once. Ecto doesn't make that decision for you. It provides the errors as a data structure containing all the relevant details, and lets the application developer decide the best way to present them.

Creating Custom Validations

The validations provided by the validate_ functions in Ecto.Changeset were designed to handle most cases that developers need. But sometimes you'll need a validation that's not provided out of the box. Ecto provides two ways to create custom validations.

Validating with validate_change

The first approach is to use the validate_change function within your validation pipeline. This function lets you supply an anonymous function that performs whatever checks you'd like to run. The anonymous function should accept two arguments: an atom representing the name of the field you're validating, and the current value for that field. If the data is incorrect, the function should return a keyword list containing the appropriate error messages; otherwise, it should return an empty list.

In this example, we'll verify that the birth_date value is in the past—we'll also allow it to be nil:

```
priv/examples/changeset_05.exs
params = %{"name" => "Thelonius Monk", "birth_date" => "2117-10-10"}
changeset =
  %Artist{}
  |> cast(params, [:name, :birth_date])
  |> validate_change(:birth_date, fn :birth_date, birth_date ->
    cond do
      is_nil(birth_date) -> []
      Date.compare(birth_date, Date.utc_today()) == :lt -> []
      true -> [birth_date: "must be in the past"]
    end
  end)
changeset.errors
#=> [birth_date: {"must be in the past", []}]
```

validate_change is an all-purpose validator that allows you to perform any sort of validation you might need. The downside is that you can end up with a lot of nested code within your pipeline. This can be tough to read if you're stringing a few of these together. You can mitigate this by moving your validation logic into a separate function. Let's walk through that now.

Validating with a Separate Function

Creating a custom validation function improves readability and also allows you to reuse your validation in multiple changesets. Custom functions work best if they can be piped along with Ecto's validation functions, so it's best to follow the same format: take a changeset as the first argument, and return the same changeset if the validation succeeds, or a new changeset with added errors if it fails.

For a first pass, we could take the validation code from the previous example, and wrap it in a function:

```
def validate_birth_date_in_the_past(changeset) do
  validate_change(changeset, :birth_date, fn :birth_date, birth_date ->
    cond do
      is_nil(birth_date) -> []
      Date.compare(birth_date, Date.utc_today()) == :lt -> []
      true -> [birth_date: "must be in the past"]
    end
  end)
end
```

This works, but it would be more useful if it could validate any date field, not just one that happened to be named birth_date. Let's rewrite it to be more generic:

```
def validate_in_the_past(changeset, field) do
  validate_change(changeset, field, fn _field, value ->
    cond do
      is_nil(value) -> []
      Date.compare(value, Date.utc_today()) == :lt -> []
      true -> [{field, "must be in the past"}]
    end
  end)
end
```

Now we're ready to put this to work. We set up our function to work like the validations that come with Ecto, so we can add it to our existing pipeline of validations:

```
params = %{"name" => "Thelonius Monk", "birth_date" => "2117-10-10"}
changeset =
  %Artist{}
  |> cast(params, [:name, :birth_date])
  |> validate_required(:name)
  |> validate_in_the_past(:birth_date)
```

This is a lot cleaner than what we had before. And because the logic was extracted out to its own named function, we can reuse it in other changesets.

Working with Constraints

Now that we've taken a look at validations, let's look at the other tool Ecto provides to ensure that data is correct: constraints.

On the surface, constraints work a lot like validations. They can be piped along with validations when building a changeset, and they check specific aspects of a changeset to make sure that the underlying data is correct. But unlike validations, constraints are enforced by the database, not by Elixir code.

As an example, consider the genres table we worked with in the last chapter. We want to be sure that each of the genre records has a unique name—we wouldn't want two records both called "jazz," for example. One approach would be to enforce this in our Elixir code: we could just check the database for a duplicate record before we try to insert a new one. That would work most of the time, but there's always the possibility of a race condition: another process could insert the duplicate record between the time that we looked for it and the time that we inserted our new record.

The only way we can be absolutely sure that we won't introduce duplicate records is if we add a unique index in the database itself. In this case, we'd want to add an index to the name column of the genre database table (we'll look at exactly how to do this in Chapter 6, Making Changes to Your Database, on page 101).

With that index in place, we can be sure that the database will prevent the creation of duplicate records. If we attempt to do so, the database will block it, and Ecto will raise an error.

In this example, we'll try to insert a Genre record for "speed polka" twice. The first call will succeed, but the second will fail:

```
priv/examples/changeset_06.exs
Repo.insert(%Genre{name: "speed polka"})

Repo.insert(%Genre{name: "speed polka"})

#=>
#=> ** (Ecto.ConstraintError) constraint error when attempting to insert
#=>  struct:
#=>
#=>     * unique: genres_name_index
#=>
#=> If you would like to convert this constraint into an error, please
#=> call unique_constraint/3 in your changeset and define the proper
#=> constraint name. The changeset has not defined any constraint.
```

Our index is working as it should, but raising an error for this condition is unwieldy. This is really a data problem, and we'd like to treat it that way. Fortunately, as the error message suggests, we can do just that. If we add a constraint to our changeset, the error will be captured in the changeset.errors field and won't cause an exception.

Like validations, constraints are functions provided by the Ecto.Changeset module, but they end with _constraint: unique_constraint, foreign_key_constraint, and so on. Let's see if we can put unique_constraint to work.

We'll insert a new genre record, then create a changeset to insert a duplicate record. We'll add unique_constraint to our changeset to make sure the name value is unique:

```
Repo.insert!(%Genre{ name: "bebop" })

params = %{"name" => "bebop"}
changeset =
  %Genre{}
  |> cast(params, [:name])
  |> validate_required(:name)
  |> validate_length(:name, min: 3)
  |> unique_constraint(:name)
changeset.errors
#=> []
```

The result is surprising: we get no error messages and the changeset says it's valid. That seems counterintuitive—we were deliberately trying to insert a duplicate record, so we should have gotten a validation error.

This illustrates the fact that constraints, unlike validations, are enforced by the database, not by our Elixir code. We haven't yet handed our changeset off to Repo, so the database has no idea what we're up to. It's only when we try to insert the record that the constraint will kick in:

```
params = %{"name" => "bebop"}
changeset =
  %Genre{}
  |> cast(params, [:name])
  |> validate_required(:name)
  |> validate_length(:name, min: 3)
  |> unique_constraint(:name)
case Repo.insert(changeset) do
  {:ok, _genre} -> IO.puts "Success!"
  {:error, changeset} -> IO.inspect changeset.errors
end
#=> [name: {"has already been taken", []}]
```

Because constraints are enforced by the database, they behave differently than validations. Ecto will always run all validations for a given changeset—even if one fails, the rest are still checked. That's usually what you want. It's more convenient to the user to show them all of the values that are incorrect at once, rather than one at a time. But constraints act like circuit breakers: if you have more than one, and one of them fails, the others won't be checked. Similarly, if any validations fail, the constraints are not checked at all. Ecto won't bother trying to send a changeset to the database if it fails validation.

This behavior can be troublesome in some situations. Imagine that your application has a lengthy user registration form, and your database has a unique index on the username column, assuring that each user has a unique username. You'd want to use unique_constraint in your changeset so that the users would get an error message if they entered a username that was already taken. But that won't get checked until all of the validations pass. If users made mistakes on other parts of the form, they'd see error messages from the failing validations. They would correct all of their mistakes, and only then would they find out that their username wasn't available. That can make for a frustrating experience.

Fortunately, Ecto provides a workaround for this situation. The unsafe_validate_unique function is a hybrid between a validation and a constraint. Like a constraint, it checks the database to see if the value already exists, but it's evaluated along with the rest of the validations, so the user will see all of the validation errors together.

The unsafe part of the function name indicates that you don't want to rely on this completely. There's still a chance that someone else could insert a duplicate value between the time that the function runs and Ecto tries to insert the record. But this allows you to give early feedback to the users that they need to pick a new username. It's rare that you'll run into the race condition that unique_constraint protects against, but you'll want to have it there anyway, just in case.

Capturing Errors

The last step of the process is sending our changeset to Repo and seeing what happens. In this section, we'll see how changesets help us track errors and report them to the user.

Looking back at our example from the beginning of the chapter, we can see the entire changeset workflow:

```elixir
priv/examples/changeset_07.exs
params = %{name: "Gene Harris"}
changeset =
  %Artist{}
  |> cast(params, [:name])
  |> validate_required([:name])

case Repo.insert(changeset) do
  {:ok, artist} -> IO.puts("Record for #{artist.name} was created.")
  {:error, changeset} -> IO.inspect(changeset.errors)
end
```

This is how we handle inserting a new record (if we were updating an existing record, we would pass the changeset into Repo.update). In either case, developers typically follow the pattern shown here: pipe the changeset through a series of validation functions then immediately hand the changeset off to the Repo without checking the valid? field of the changeset. This is safe to do: if Repo sees that the changeset has validation errors, it won't send anything to the database. It will return :error along with the changeset, as seen in the second half of the preceding case statement.

You could check for validation errors yourself before calling insert or update, but you'd still need to check for :error coming back from the call to Repo. It's possible that the database will catch a problem with your data that you forgot to write a validation for, so it usually makes the most sense to concentrate all of your error handling in one place.

If the operation succeeds, Ecto will return :ok along with a struct representing the inserted record. In this case, the artist value would have the name we provided ("Gene Harris") as well as any values that were added by the database (the ID, the timestamps, and so forth).

If the operation fails, you'll get :error with a new changeset that has all of the data you added, plus any new error messages resulting from the insert operation. This will include validation errors, constraint violations, and the like. As we saw earlier, errors take the form of a keyword list, where the keys represent the fields of your schema, and the values contain text representations of the error messages:

```elixir
params = %{name: nil}
changeset =
  %Artist{}
  |> cast(params, [:name])
  |> validate_required([:name])
```

```
case Repo.insert(changeset) do
  {:ok, artist} -> IO.puts("Record for #{artist.name} was created.")
  {:error, changeset} -> IO.inspect(changeset.errors)
end
#=> [name: {"can't be blank", [validation: :required]}]
```

At this point, the changeset has a lot of critical information: it knows the
changes the user tried to make, what kind of record it's working with, and
what the error messages are. This makes it a handy data structure for the
front end of your application to report to the user what happened. For
example, the phoenix_ecto Hex package implements protocols defined in Phoenix
so that changesets can be used by the form-rendering functions. See Chapter
8, Working with Changesets and Phoenix Forms, on page 131 recipe for more
details.

Using Changesets Without Schemas

Up to this point, our changesets have been based on the schemas defined in
our music_db app: Artist, Genre, and so forth. But changesets don't actually need
Ecto schemas—they can be created with plain maps that define field names
and types. This means that you can leverage the casting, filtering, and validation features of changesets, even if the data is not being persisted in a
database.

Let's say that our application will have an "Advanced Search" feature. We'll
allow users to specify a number of different fields to help them find what
they're looking for: artist names, album titles, dates, and the like. We can
validate the form using the features of Ecto.Changeset, and then report any errors
back to the user. Recall that changesets are just data structures and have a
lot of utility before they are ever sent to the database.

The first step is to set up a map that defines the shape of the data that we
want to process. The keys should be the field names, and the values should
be the data types for each field. You can use any of the data types supported
by the Ecto.Schema module. Here's what we might use for our "Advanced Search"
feature:

priv/examples/changeset_08.exs
```
form = %{artist_name: :string, album_title: :string,
        artist_birth_date: :date, album_release_date: :date,
        genre: :string}
```

We can use the map to create a new changeset, then cast and validate as
usual:

```
form = %{artist_name: :string, album_title: :string,
         artist_birth_date: :date, album_release_date: :date,
         genre: :string}

# user data - they only provided one value
params = %{"artist_name" => "Ella Fitzgerald", "album_title" => "",
"artist_birth_date" => "",  "album_release_date" => "",
"genre" => ""}

changeset =
  {%{}, form}
  |> cast(params, Map.keys(form))
  |> validate_in_the_past(:artist_birth_date)
  |> validate_in_the_past(:album_release_date)

if changeset.valid? do
  # execute the advanced search
else
  # show changeset.errors to the user
end
```

This example has nothing to do with database tables, but there's quite a lot of utility in the Ecto.Changeset functions for casting and validating data. If you need to process data in this way, you might think about using Ecto to help, even if your app doesn't use a database.

Working with Associations

So far, all of our changesets have been using a single schema. But you will often need to update associated records as well as parent records at the same time. Ecto provides a number of options for updating associated records, each serving a particular purpose depending on where your data is coming from and how you want it updated. In this section, we'll look at the various ways we can insert and update Artist records along with associated Album records.

Updating a Single Associated Record

When making changes to child records, the first question to ask yourself is if you want to make changes to an individual child record, or if you want to change the entire collection of associated records at once. If you want to work with individual records, it's usually best to make changes outside of a changeset. As we'll see shortly, the functions provided by Ecto.Changeset for working with associations are geared toward the collection as a whole. For individual records, Ecto has other options.

For example, to add a new record to an association, the Ecto.build_assoc function is a great choice. You give it the parent record and the name of the association, and it generates a new child record, with the foreign key set to the parent record. Here's how we might add a new album to our collection of albums by Miles Davis:

```
priv/examples/changeset_09.exs
artist = Repo.get_by(Artist, name: "Miles Davis")
new_album = Ecto.build_assoc(artist, :albums)
#=> %MusicDB.Album{artist_id: 1, ...}
```

We've truncated some of the output to make it more readable, but the important part is visible. The new_album struct has its foreign key artist_id set to the id of our artist record.

We can also add any fields that we'd like set in the new record as options to build_assoc. Here we add the title of the new album:

```
artist = Repo.get_by(Artist, name: "Miles Davis")
album = Ecto.build_assoc(artist, :albums, title: "Miles Ahead")
#=> %MusicDB.Album{artist_id: 1, title: "Miles Ahead", ...}
```

Note that this does not insert the album into the database—we need to talk to Repo to do that, so let's do that now:

```
artist = Repo.get_by(Artist, name: "Miles Davis")
album = Ecto.build_assoc(artist, :albums, title: "Miles Ahead")
Repo.insert(album)
#=> {:ok, %MusicDB.Album{id: 6, title: "Miles Ahead", artist_id: 1, ...}}
```

Everything worked and we got our now-familiar tuple of :ok along with the newly inserted record. If we reload our Artist record and preload the albums associations, we'll see the new Album record, along with the other two records that were part of our initial dataset:

```
artist = Repo.one(from a in Artist, where: a.name == "Miles Davis",
  preload: :albums)
Enum.map(artist.albums, &(&1.title))
#=> ["Miles Ahead", "Cookin' At The Plugged Nickel", "Kind Of Blue"]
```

To update, we could create a changeset as we saw in the previous section, and we could delete it using Repo.delete or Repo.delete_all, depending on our needs. For changing associated records, you only need to use changesets if you want to update the entire collection at once. We'll explore exactly how to do that next.

Associations Using Internal Data

When we looked at casting and filtering at the beginning of this chapter, we took different approaches depending on whether or not the data we were using was generated in our application code, or if it came from an external source. We make a similar distinction when working with associations. We'll start with internal data using Ecto.Changeset.put_assoc then later use Ecto.Changeset.cast_assoc to work with external data.

Before we continue, you should run mix ecto.reset in your music_db app to get everything back to a pristine state. We'll run this a few times throughout the rest of the chapter so we can more easily track the changes we're making.

We're going to add the album "Miles Ahead" as we did in the previous section, but this time we'll use the put_assoc function from Ecto.Changeset rather than build_assoc and observe the differences.

put_assoc takes a changeset, the name of the association, and the records we want to put into the association. Like many of the functions in Ecto.Changeset, put_assoc takes a changeset as its first parameter, allowing it to be piped into the cast and validation stages. But we need to consider a few extra things. Let's see what happens if we try to add "Miles Ahead" using put_assoc:

```
priv/examples/changeset_10.exs
changeset = Repo.get_by(Artist, name: "Miles Davis")
  |> change
  |> put_assoc(:albums, [%Album{title: "Miles Ahead"}])
Repo.update(changeset)
#=> ** (RuntimeError) attempting to cast or change association `albums`
#=> from `MusicDB.Artist` that was not loaded. Please preload your
#=> associations before manipulating them through changesets
```

We're off to a bad start. We created a new changeset by passing our artist record to the change function (recall that this is the usual way to create a changeset when working with internal data). We then tried to pass that changeset to put_assoc, along with our new list of Album structs, and it blew up.

The problem is that we want to make changes to the albums association of our artist record, but Ecto doesn't know the current state of this association because we haven't preloaded it.

Let's add a call to preload, then see what happens:

```
changeset = Repo.get_by(Artist, name: "Miles Davis")
  |> Repo.preload(:albums)
  |> change
  |> put_assoc(:albums, [%Album{title: "Miles Ahead"}])
Repo.update(changeset)
#=> ** (RuntimeError) you are attempting to change relation :albums of
#=> MusicDB.Artist but the `:on_replace` option of
#=> this relation is set to `:raise`.
#=> ...
```

We got a little further, but we still got an error message. And it's a lengthy one too: we've truncated the actual output here, but Ecto provides a detailed explanation of what the problem is.

The trouble lies in the difference between build_assoc and put_assoc. With build_assoc we're creating a new Album struct that we (most likely) will be adding to the list of albums already associated with the Artist record for Miles Davis. By contrast, put_assoc works on the entire collection as whole. This line of code:

```
|> put_assoc(:albums, [%Album{title: "Miles Ahead"}])
```

is effectively saying "replace the current list of albums associated with Miles Davis with this single album called 'Miles Ahead'." We need to let Ecto know what to do with the old records when we replace them with new ones.

The functions used to add associations to schemas (has_many, belongs_to, and the like) all take an optional argument called :on_replace. This is used to tell Ecto how to handle any existing associated records when we're doing a replacement, as we're doing now. This option can be set to one of five different values:

- :raise—This is the default behavior, and it's what we just saw in the preceding example: Ecto raises an error. This will happen if you don't provide one of the other values defined here.

- :mark_as_invalid—This will tell Ecto to add a validation error to the changeset's errors field. The operation will still not succeed, but you'll just get a changeset error rather than a crash.

- :nilify—With this option, the foreign key of the associated record will be set to nil. For example, the album record for "Kind Of Blue" currently has the artist_id set to 1, the id for the Artist record for Miles Davis. If we use :nilify and call put_assoc, the artist_id for "Kind Of Blue" would be set to nil—the record would still exist, but it wouldn't be connected to any Artist record. That might be problematic depending on the nature of your database.

- :update—This option can only be used with has_one and belongs_to associations, and causes Ecto to update the associated record with the values provided by the update.

- :delete—This tells Ecto to delete any child records currently associated with the parent record that aren't part of the new collection. Use this option with care, as the deletions are permanent.

Which option you choose depends on your application, and how you want to handle the new data. If you do indeed want to replace the whole collection with put_assoc you have to decide what to do with the records you're not keeping. :nilify will keep the records in the database, but they'll no longer be associated with any parent record. :delete will remove the records permanently, making it a risky option.

In our case, we just wanted to add a new album to the existing group of albums by Miles Davis, so put_assoc was not a good fit: build_assoc would have been a better choice. If we really wanted to use put_assoc, we'd have to pass a list of all the existing albums, plus our new one—this is a little convoluted, but it would work:

```
artist =
  Repo.get_by(Artist, name: "Miles Davis")
  |> Repo.preload(:albums)
artist
|> change
|> put_assoc(:albums, [%Album{title: "Miles Ahead"} | artist.albums])
|> Repo.update
```

When inserting new parent records and child records together, working with put_assoc is more straightforward:

```
%Artist{name: "Eliane Elias"}
|> change
|> put_assoc(:albums, [%Album{title: "Made In Brazil"}])
|> Repo.insert
```

Because we're inserting a new Artist record, there are no preexisting child records to worry about, and the on_replace behavior won't be a factor.

So far, we've been using Album structs when adding associated records, but put_assoc can also work with maps and keyword lists. The following two snippets will have exactly the same effect as the previous one:

```
# adding an album with a map
%Artist{name: "Eliane Elias"}
|> change
|> put_assoc(:albums, [%{title: "Made In Brazil"}])
|> Repo.insert

# adding an album with a keyword list
%Artist{name: "Eliane Elias"}
|> change
|> put_assoc(:albums, [[title: "Made In Brazil"]])
|> Repo.insert
```

With put_assoc, you can present the records as structs, maps, or keyword lists, whichever is most convenient.

Associations Using External Data

We'll now look at creating a changeset with associations when the data comes from an external source: forms presented to the user, an uploaded spreadsheet, data posted to an API endpoint, and so on. Earlier we saw that we create new changesets using change or cast, depending on where the data came from. Similarly, we use put_assoc for internal data, as we saw in the last section, or cast_assoc for external data. In this section, we'll look at some examples using cast_assoc.

Creating New Records with Associations

Let's start with the case of adding a new parent record, with new child records. As we did when learning about cast, we'll assume that the raw data is coming to us as a map of strings. And as before, let's reset our data so our previous experiments are wiped away: mix ecto.reset

To cast the association into a changeset, Ecto expects the map to have a key matching the association name—the value should contains the values for the child records. For a has_many association, which we're using here, the value should be a list of maps, one map per record. For has_one or belongs_to, the value would just be a single map.

cast_assoc works similarly to put_assoc. It takes a changeset and the name of the association to cast. Let's create a map of values, set up a new changeset that casts the association, then peek at the changes:

```
priv/examples/changeset_11.exs
params = %{"name" => "Esperanza Spalding",
  "albums" => [%{"title" => "Junjo"}]}
changeset =
  %Artist{}
  |> cast(params, [:name])
  |> cast_assoc(:albums)
changeset.changes
```

When we try to run this code, the output is surprising:

```
** (UndefinedFunctionError) function MusicDB.Album.changeset/2 is
undefined or private. Did you mean one of:

     * __changeset__/0
```

The error message is telling us that Ecto was looking for a function called changeset in our MusicDB.Album module. This gives us a clue about what's going on behind the scenes of cast_assoc. It is looking at our code to generate a new changeset for the child record we want to insert. A peek at the documentation confirms this:

> If the parameter does not contain an ID, the parameter data will be passed to changeset/2 with a new struct and become an insert operation.

Ecto wants to use changesets that we provide to create the child records. This is a good thing: it will allow us to add validations as well as any custom param handling that might be needed. As the error message indicates, we haven't defined a changeset function in our Album module, so let's do that now. For this example, it can be a short one:

```
# add this to lib/music_db/album.ex
def changeset(album, params) do
  album
  |> cast(params, [:title])
  |> validate_required([:title])
end
```

We'll also want to add import Ecto.Changeset to the top of the file, so we can call cast and validate_required directly, without including the Changeset module name.

Now we can try our code again:

```
params = %{"name" => "Esperanza Spalding",
  "albums" => [%{"title" => "Junjo"}]}
changeset =
  %Artist{}
  |> cast(params, [:name])
  |> cast_assoc(:albums)
changeset.changes
#=> %{albums: [#Ecto.Changeset<action: :insert,
#=>   changes: %{title: "Junjo"}, errors: [],
#=>   data: #MusicDB.Album<>, valid?: true>],
#=>   name: "Esperanza Spalding"}
```

That looks better. And as we look more closely at the output, we can see that our changes include an embedded changeset for our album child record: a changeset within a changeset!

As discussed earlier, it's convention in Ecto to have one or more changeset functions in our schema modules, so it makes sense that cast_assoc would look there first. But you can override this behavior by adding the with: option to cast_assoc. You can use this to tell Ecto which function to invoke when it needs to generate a changeset for child records. Like the changeset function we just defined, this function needs to take a schema struct representing the child record and a map of params. And of course it should return a changeset:

```
|> cast_assoc(:albums, with: &SomeModule.some_function/2)
```

In most cases, it will make sense to have your changeset function defined in the schema module, but when you don't, the with: option gives you an escape hatch.

Updating Records with Associations

We just looked at how to work with cast_assoc when creating a new parent record. Let's now look at what happens when we're updating an existing record. Before we do, let's reset our database one more time to clean the slate:

```
mix ecto.reset
```

Now let's make some changes to the Artist and Album records for Bill Evans. If you've just reset your database, you should have an Artist record and two Album records. We can confirm that with this bit of code:

```
artist = Repo.get_by(Artist, name: "Bill Evans")
  |> Repo.preload(:albums)
IO.inspect Enum.map(artist.albums, &({&1.id, &1.title}))
#=> [{4, "Portrait In Jazz"}, {3, "You Must Believe In Spring"}]
```

It's OK if the ids in your output don't match the ones shown here, but the titles should be the same.

Now let's make some changes to the collection of albums using cast_assoc. Recall that, like put_assoc, cast_assoc works on the entire collection of associated records, so we'll need to add the on_replace option to our has_many call. We'll use nilify for now, as that will keep any discarded child records in the database so we can see what happens to them. Open up lib/music_db/artist.ex and change the has_many :albums line so it looks like this:

```
has_many :albums, Album, on_replace: :nilify
```

Now we will set up the params to modify the album collection. We are going to make several different kinds of changes at once, so that we can see how Ecto handles them:

```
portrait = Repo.get_by(Album, title: "Portrait In Jazz")
kind_of_blue = Repo.get_by(Album, title: "Kind Of Blue")
params = %{"albums" =>
  [
    %{"title" => "Explorations"},
    %{"title" => "Portrait In Jazz (remastered)", "id" => portrait.id},
    %{"title" => "Kind Of Blue", "id" => kind_of_blue.id}
  ]
}
```

The params we've created set up three different kinds of operations.

First, we've got a new album "Explorations" that isn't in the database yet. Ecto will perform an insert operation for this record, and make it part of the :albums association for our Artist record.

Next, we have an existing record "Portrait In Jazz" that is already associated with the "Bill Evans" artist record. The id value indicates that this record is already in the database, but we're making a change to the title. Ecto will update the existing record with the new title.

Finally, we have an odd case. There's already an album record for "Kind Of Blue," as indicated by the id value, but this album is currently associated with Miles Davis, not Bill Evans. In this case, Ecto will treat this as a new record. It will ignore the given id and create a new record, using any other values provided in the given map.

You may have noticed that there's a fourth hidden operation created by these params. If you recall when we looked at the albums we have for Bill Evans, "You Must Believe In Spring" was in the list. We have not included that album in the params shown previously. Ecto will look to the on_replace: setting of the association to determine how to handle this. We've set it to :nilify so Ecto will update the record for "You Must Believe In Spring," setting its artist_id value to nil. This will keep the record in the database, but it'll no longer be associated with Bill Evans. Had we set on_replace: to :delete, the record would've been deleted.

Now we can cast these params into a changeset, run an update, and see if everything ended up as we predicted:

```elixir
portrait = Repo.get_by(Album, title: "Portrait In Jazz")
kind_of_blue = Repo.get_by(Album, title: "Kind Of Blue")
params = %{"albums" =>
  [
    %{"title" => "Explorations"},
    %{"title" => "Portrait In Jazz (remastered)", "id" => portrait.id},
    %{"title" => "Kind Of Blue", "id" => kind_of_blue.id}
  ]
}
artist = Repo.get_by(Artist, name: "Bill Evans")
  |> Repo.preload(:albums)
{:ok, artist} =
  artist
  |> cast(params, [])
  |> cast_assoc(:albums)
  |> Repo.update
Enum.map(artist.albums, &({&1.id, &1.title}))
#=> [{6, "Explorations"}, {4, "Portrait In Jazz (remastered)"},
#=>  {7, "Kind Of Blue"}]
```

The end result was as expected:

- We created a new "Explorations" album, associated with Bill Evans

- The "Portrait In Jazz" record was updated in place with a new title (compare the id to the one we got earlier—they should be the same)

- We created a new record with the title "Kind Of Blue"—even though we passed the id of the record associated with Miles Davis, Ecto created a new record

- "You Must Believe In Spring" is no longer a part of the albums collection for Bill Evans

We can confirm the presence of two "Kind Of Blue" albums:

```
Repo.all(from a in Album, where: a.title == "Kind Of Blue")
|> Enum.map(&({&1.id, &1.title}))
#=> [{1, "Kind Of Blue"}, {7, "Kind Of Blue"}]
```

and that "You Must Believe In Spring" is still in the database:

```
Repo.all(from a in Album, where: a.title == "You Must Believe In Spring")
|> Enum.map(&({&1.id, &1.title, &1.artist_id}))
#=> [{3, "You Must Believe In Spring", nil}]
```

Our :nilify setting for on_replace did the trick, and the record is no longer associated with any Artist record.

Best Practices for Associations

We've covered a lot of ground in this section. Changesets have a lot of support for associations and can be used in many ways. It's sometimes confusing to know what approach to use. Let's sum up some rules and best practices for you to keep in mind as you start integrating these techniques into your own apps.

The first thing to ask yourself is whether you want to work with individual child records, or if you want to work with the collection as a whole. If you're working with individual records (for example, inserting or deleting a single child record), it's usually easiest to work with the child record separate from the parent record. build_assoc can help you create new child records for a given parent record, and you can perform updates and deletes by loading the child record and using the update and delete functions provided by Repo.

If you want to work with the collection as a whole, you'll need to think about what you want to do with records that are removed or replaced when the collection is updated. Review the documentation about your options, then set the on_replace option for the association in your schema definition.

Then you need to consider where the data is coming from. If the data is coming from an external source, then you'll want to use cast_assoc. Behind the scenes, cast_assoc uses changesets you supply to cast and validate the data, giving you a lot of control over how the data is imported and checked for errors.

If the data is being generated by you in your application code, you can use put_assoc to add data structures directly. And don't forget that if you're inserting new records of internally generated data, you can bypass changesets altogether and use Repo.insert to add parent and child records all at once. See the end of the last chapter for an example.

put_assoc is also a good choice when you're managing parent and child records separately, even when working with external data. You could, for example, use changesets to create/update/delete the child records on their own, then use put_assoc in a separate changeset to update the collection on the parent record. This is often a great way to work with many-to-many associations.

Ecto gives you a lot of choices. Some will work better than others, depending on the situation. If your code feels clumsy, or too complicated, try another approach and see if it works better.

Wrapping Up

We did a deep dive into the Ecto.Changeset module, and saw the many functions it provides to help us manage making changes to our data. With its support for associations, changesets can modify related records across multiple tables, allowing us to make complicated changes with just a few lines of code.

But sometimes, we need to make even more complex changes. We might need to change several unrelated records and make sure that they all change together. For these types of situations, Ecto gives us transactions and the Multi module—we'll take a look at those next.

## CHAPTER 5

Making Multiple Changes
with Transactions and Multi

Throughout this book, we've been working with one database operation at a time. But there are times when you have multiple operations that need to be treated as a group: they all need to succeed together, or fail together.

A classic example is transferring money between two bank accounts. If we want to transfer $10 from Bob's account and put it in Alice's account (it's always Bob and Alice for some reason), we have to perform two updates: reducing Bob's balance by 10 and increasing Alice's balance by 10. But what would happen if the update to Bob's balance succeeded, but the update to Alice's balance failed? The accounts would be out of sync, and the $10 would effectively be missing.

Databases need integrity, and that means *transactions*. Transactions allow you to group operations together so you can be certain that they will all succeed, or all fail.

Databases differ in how they implement this feature, but the general rule is that you send a command indicating that you're starting a transaction, run your operations, then send another command indicating that you're ending the transaction. If any of the operations within the transaction fail, the database executes a *rollback*. A rollback is the database equivalent of the "undo" feature in your text editor: the database restores any records changed within the transaction back to the state they were in before the transaction began.

Ecto supports transactions through the Repo.transaction function. You can execute this function in two ways. The first way is to provide another function that contains the operations you'd like to execute. The second way is to use

Ecto.Multi, a data structure consisting of a queue of operations to be run within a transaction.

In this chapter, we'll look at both options separately. We'll start with functions, then take a look at the Ecto.Multi module, and discuss when you might want to use one rather than the other.

Running Transactions with Functions

The first way to run Repo.transaction is by passing in a function containing the operations you'd like to run within the transaction. This can be an anonymous function or a named function defined elsewhere. This seems like a good idea—we're functional programmers, and this approach will let us keep using functions. Let's try it out.

To illustrate how this works, we're going to introduce a new database table, and a module to go with it. Imagine that we've decided that we want to keep a log of the changes we make to our database. Every time we make a change, we'll insert a new record into a logs table. We'll use functions in the MusicDB.Log module to create changesets for logging the different operations that we want to perform. It's not too fancy, but it will suffice for our purposes here. Take a peek at the lib/music_db/log.ex module if you're curious to see the details.

Here's what we would do if we wanted to insert a new Artist record, and log the change:

```
priv/examples/transactions_01.exs
artist = %Artist{name: "Johnny Hodges"}
Repo.insert(artist)
Repo.insert(Log.changeset_for_insert(artist))
```

That would work most of the time, but we want to be absolutely certain that both of these inserts succeed: we don't want to add a new Log record if the Artist insert didn't go through, and if the Log insert fails, we want to back out the Artist insert. We can do this by wrapping the two calls in an anonymous function, and passing that function directly to the Repo.transaction function:

```
artist = %Artist{name: "Johnny Hodges"}
Repo.transaction(fn ->
  Repo.insert!(artist)
  Repo.insert!(Log.changeset_for_insert(artist))
end)
#=> {:ok, %MusicDB.Log{ ...}}
```

When a transaction succeeds (as this one did), the transaction function returns a tuple consisting of :ok and the return value of the passed-in function. In this case, the last line of the function inserts the Log struct, so we get the return value of that operation: %MusicDB.Log{...}.

If an error occurs anywhere in the transaction, the database rolls back all of the changes that it performed up to that point, and the transaction function itself raises the error. We can demonstrate this by trying to insert nil for the second operation:

```
artist = %Artist{name: "Ben Webster"}
Repo.transaction(fn ->
  Repo.insert!(artist)
  Repo.insert!(nil) # <-- this will fail
end)
#=> ** (FunctionClauseError) no function clause matching in
#=> Ecto.Repo.Schema.insert/4
```

Elixir rightfully complained about our attempt to insert nil and raised the error. We expect that any changes performed within transaction got rolled back, and we can verify that by making sure no Artist record now exists for Ben Webster:

```
Repo.get_by(Artist, name: "Ben Webster")
# => nil
```

Our transaction worked. The failure of the second insert forced a rollback of the first insert. We're back to where we were before we started.

Forcing a Rollback Within a Transaction

Notice that we've been using insert! with a bang, rather than insert. The two functions are identical, except for one crucial difference: insert will return {:error, value} if the insert fails, but insert! will raise an error. This is a convention that's used in many Elixir libraries, and it's essential when executing transaction with a function.

The documentation for Repo.transaction says this:

> If an unhandled error occurs the transaction will be rolled back and the error will bubble up from the transaction function.

This means that only unhandled errors will trigger the rollback behavior—a return value of {:error, value} from one of the operations isn't going to cut it.

We can demonstrate this by rewriting our transaction so we're inserting changesets rather than schema structs. If we pass an invalid changeset to insert (without the bang) it will return an :error tuple without raising an error. We'll add some debug output so we can see exactly what's going on:

```
priv/examples/transactions_02.exs
cs =
  %Artist{name: nil}
  |> Ecto.Changeset.change()
  |> Ecto.Changeset.validate_required([:name])
Repo.transaction(fn ->
  case Repo.insert(cs) do
    {:ok, _artist} -> IO.puts("Artist insert succeeded")
    {:error, _value} -> IO.puts("Artist insert failed")
  end
  case Repo.insert(Log.changeset_for_insert(cs)) do
    {:ok, _log} -> IO.puts("Log insert succeeded")
    {:error, _value} -> IO.puts("Log insert failed")
  end
end)
```

We start by creating an intentionally invalid changeset: we pass in nil for the name field, then add a validation declaring that name is required. This should give us :error when we try to insert it. Then we try to insert the changeset and a separate Log changeset within the transaction. The case statements help us to see how each of those operations fare. Here's what happens when we run this:

```
# => Artist insert failed
# => Log insert succeeded
# => {:ok :ok}
```

This is exactly what we *don't* want when working with transactions. The first insert failed, but because we used insert rather than insert! the function returned the tuple {:error, _value} instead of raising an error. If we want to trigger a rollback, we have to raise an Elixir error, and passing an invalid changeset to insert won't do that. You have to use insert! (with a bang) instead. Because we used insert, the transaction continued, and the second insert succeeded. Our database is now in an incorrect state: we have a log record for an insert that didn't actually happen.

One workaround for this behavior is to use the Repo.rollback function. Calling this function will abort the transaction and roll back any changes made so far, just as if an error had occurred. When you call rollback, the transaction function returns {:error, value} where value is the argument passed to the rollback function. With this in mind, we can rewrite the previous example to get the behavior we want:

```
cs = Ecto.Changeset.change(%Artist{name: nil})
  |> Ecto.Changeset.validate_required([:name])
Repo.transaction(fn ->
  case Repo.insert(cs) do
    {:ok, _artist} -> IO.puts("Artist insert succeeded")
    {:error, _value} -> Repo.rollback("Artist insert failed")
  end
```

```
  case Repo.insert(Log.changeset_for_insert(cs)) do
    {:ok, _log} -> IO.puts("Log insert succeeded")
    {:error, _value} -> Repo.rollback("Log insert failed")
  end
end)
# => {:error, "Artist insert failed"}
```

That's better. This time, the first insert failed as expected so the rest of the transaction didn't run. The transaction function returned an :error tuple with the value we provided.

Executing Non-Database Operations Within a Transaction

With this knowledge in hand, we can see an opportunity to expand transactions to include non-database operations. Imagine that our app uses an external search engine, such as Elasticsearch. Whenever we change the database, we want to update our search engine as well. But it's important to keep the database and the search engine in sync: if the database changes fail, we don't want to update the search engine, and if the search engine update fails, we want to roll back the changes to the database.

To explore this scenario, our MusicDB app has a MusicDB.SearchEngine module that handles search engine updates via its update function. This is just a placeholder module—our sample app doesn't include a real search engine, so the module's functions just simulate the behavior.

To update the search engine along with the changes to the database, we call the appropriate functions from within the transaction:

```
priv/examples/transactions_03.exs
artist = %Artist{name: "Johnny Hodges"}
Repo.transaction(fn ->
  artist_record = Repo.insert!(artist)
  Repo.insert!(Log.changeset_for_insert(artist_record))
  SearchEngine.update!(artist_record)
end)
```

Provided that our update! function raises an error if it fails, this will do what we want: if either of the insert! calls fail, the search engine update won't run. And if the search engine update fails, Ecto will roll back the database changes and the transaction function will bubble up the error.

Of course, Ecto has no knowledge of how our search engine works, so it would be impossible for it to roll back changes to the search engine. This means that you should run all of your database operations first, then run any non-database operations: you don't want those to run until you're sure the database operations succeeded.

Drawbacks of Using Functions

Running transactions with functions works reasonably well, but it has some drawbacks.

The most serious problem, demonstrated in the last section, is that *we have to be careful that we call Repo functions in the correct way.* Calling insert rather than insert! broke the behavior we were trying to achieve. The compiler can't help us with something like this, so one missed character could put our database into a bad state.

Another problem is that *anonymous functions are not composable:* this limits their reusability. Our last example made changes to an Artist record, saved a log of the change, and updated the search engine. It's possible that in another part of the app we might want to update the artist's albums along with the artist record. It would be nice to take the logic we already have and just add to it, but our anonymous function doesn't lend itself to being extended in that way.

There's still another problem. *We don't have good visibility into exactly what went wrong when a transaction fails.* Recall how much code we had to add when we wanted to see where a failure occurred:

```
priv/examples/transactions_04.exs
cs = Ecto.Changeset.change(%Artist{name: nil})
  |> Ecto.Changeset.validate_required([:name])
Repo.transaction(fn ->
  case Repo.insert(cs) do
    {:ok, _artist} -> IO.puts("Artist insert succeeded")
    {:error, _value} -> Repo.rollback("Artist insert failed")
  end
  case Repo.insert(Log.changeset_for_insert(cs)) do
    {:ok, _log} -> IO.puts("Log insert succeeded")
    {:error, _value} -> Repo.rollback("Log insert failed")
  end
end)
```

That's a lot of extra code for only two Repo calls.

Fortunately, there's a better way. The Ecto.Multi module can help us out with all of these issues. We'll explore that option in the next section.

Running Transactions with Ecto.Multi

The other way to use Repo.transaction is pass in an Ecto.Multi struct, rather than a function. Ecto.Multi allows you to group your database operations into a data structure. When handed to the transaction function, the Multi's operations run in order, and if any of them fail, all of the others are rolled back.

Let's take a look at an earlier example where we ran a transaction with an anonymous function:

```
priv/examples/transactions_05.exs
artist = %Artist{name: "Johnny Hodges"}
Repo.transaction(fn ->
  Repo.insert!(artist)
  Repo.insert!(Log.changeset_for_insert(artist))
end)
```

Here's how we can rewrite it using Multi:

```
alias Ecto.Multi

artist = %Artist{name: "Johnny Hodges"}
multi =
  Multi.new
  |> Multi.insert(:artist, artist)
  |> Multi.insert(:log, Log.changeset_for_insert(artist))
Repo.transaction(multi)
```

There's a lot here, so let's walk through it.

We start by creating a new Multi with the new function. The Ecto team recommends using this approach rather than trying to create the struct directly; that is, don't try to write something like multi = %Multi{}. The exact structure of Ecto.Multi is subject to future change. Calling new ensures that the struct will come back to you properly initialized. If you create the struct directly, you're on your own.

We then add the two insert operations by piping the Multi into the insert function. The Ecto.Multi module has several functions that mirror the database operation functions in Repo: insert, update, delete, and so on. Each of the operations that we add to the Multi must have a unique name—that's what the :artist and :log atoms are for. After that, we pass exactly what we would pass to the Repo.insert function: an Artist struct for the first call, and our Log changeset for the second.

For this example, we don't have any other options we need to include in our insert calls, but if we did, we could add them here. The functions in Multi can accept the same options as their counterparts in Repo, so anything you might send to Repo.insert can be sent to Multi.insert as well.

At this point, we still haven't touched the database. We just have a list of operations stored in the Multi struct. When we finally pass the struct to Repo.transaction, the database begins executing the operations queued in the Multi. The return value, however, is different than what we get when we pass in a function:

```
Repo.transaction(multi)
#=> {:ok,
#=>   %{
#=>     artist: %MusicDB.Artist{...}
#=>     log: %MusicDB.Log{...}
#=>   }}
```

The transaction succeeded, so we get a tuple with :ok and a map. The keys in the map are the unique names we provided to each operation in the Multi (:artist and :log in this case). The values are the return values for each of those operations. This makes it easy for us to grab the return values of any or all of the operations we ran. In this case, both of the operations were inserts, so we get structs representing our newly inserted records.

Capturing Errors with Multi

Here's where the two approaches really diverge. If an error occurs in a Multi, we get detailed information on where the error occurred, and what happened just before. Let's take a look.

Examining the Return Value

To see this in action, let's create a new Multi that performs an update on the Artist record we just inserted, then tries to insert an invalid changeset:

```
priv/examples/transactions_06.exs
artist = Repo.get_by(Artist, name: "Johnny Hodges")
artist_changeset = Artist.changeset(artist,
  %{name: "John Cornelius Hodges"})
invalid_changeset = Artist.changeset(%Artist{},
  %{name: nil})
multi =
  Multi.new
  |> Multi.update(:artist, artist_changeset)
  |> Multi.insert(:invalid, invalid_changeset)
Repo.transaction(multi)
#=> {:error, :invalid,
#=>   #Ecto.Changeset<
#=>     action: :insert,
#=>     changes: %{},
#=>     errors: [name: {"can't be blank", [validation: :required]}],
#=>     data: #MusicDB.Artist<>,
#=>     valid?: false
#=>   >, %{}}
```

This time, the Multi failed, so we get a tuple with four items: the :error atom, the name of the operation that failed (:invalid), the value that caused the failure (in this case, the invalid changeset, with a populated errors field), and a map containing the changes so far. The database will have already rolled back these changes, but Ecto provides them for you to inspect if needed.

The benefit of this arrangement is that this single return value tells if we succeeded, or, if we failed, exactly *where* we failed. This means that we can use pattern matching to respond to each of the success or failure scenarios separately:

```
case Repo.transaction(multi) do
  {:ok, _results} ->
    IO.puts "Operations were successful."
  {:error, :artist, changeset, _changes} ->
    IO.puts "Artist update failed"
    IO.inspect changeset.errors
  {:error, :invalid, changeset, _changes} ->
    IO.puts "Invalid operation failed"
    IO.inspect changeset.errors
end
```

That's a lot cleaner than what we had when we were using anonymous functions with Repo.transaction. Here we used a single case statement as our responses were fairly short. But you could also use pattern-matched functions if you needed more complex responses.

Examining the List of Changes So Far

The last value of the returned tuple is supposed to be a list of changes that occurred before the error happened. Let's take another look at what we got in the last example:

```
artist = Repo.get_by(Artist, name: "Johnny Hodges")
artist_changeset = Artist.changeset(artist,
  %{name: "John Cornelius Hodges"})
invalid_changeset = Artist.changeset(%Artist{},
  %{name: nil})
multi =
  Multi.new
  |> Multi.update(:artist, artist_changeset)
  |> Multi.insert(:invalid, invalid_changeset)
Repo.transaction(multi)
#=> {:error, :invalid,
#=>   #Ecto.Changeset<
#=>     action: :insert,
#=>     changes: %{},
#=>     errors: [name: {"can't be blank", [validation: :required]}],
#=>     data: #MusicDB.Artist<>,
#=>     valid?: false
#=>   >, %{}}
```

We got an empty map—that seems surprising. The return value told us that the second operation in the Multi failed, so we would expect to see the result of the first operation in the list of changes so far.

This is because Ecto doesn't like to waste the database's time. If the Multi contains operations that use changesets, Ecto first checks to make sure all the changesets are valid. If any are not, Ecto won't bother running the transaction at all. It just flags the invalid changeset and sends it back to us in the return value. There's no need to trouble the database with an invalid changeset.

Let's try a different example so we can see something besides an empty map. We'll create a new Multi that starts with a successful update. We'll then force an error by trying to insert a new %Genre{} record with a name that already exists in the database (as you might recall from Working with Constraints, on page 71, the genres table has a unique index on the name column).

```
artist = Repo.get_by(Artist, name: "Johnny Hodges")
artist_changeset = Artist.changeset(artist,
  %{name: "John Cornelius Hodges"})
genre_changeset =
  %Genre{}
  |> Ecto.Changeset.cast(%{name: "jazz"}, [:name])
  |> Ecto.Changeset.unique_constraint(:name)
multi =
  Multi.new
  |> Multi.update(:artist, artist_changeset)
  |> Multi.insert(:bad_genre, genre_changeset)
Repo.transaction(multi)
#=> {:error, :bad_genre, #Ecto.Changeset< ... >,
#=> %{
#=>   artist: %MusicDB.Artist{
#=>     __meta__: #Ecto.Schema.Metadata<:loaded, "artists">,
#=>     albums: #Ecto.Association.NotLoaded<association
#=>       :albums is not loaded>,
#=>     birth_date: nil,
#=>     death_date: nil,
#=>     id: 4,
#=>     inserted_at: ~N[2018-03-23 14:02:28],
#=>     name: "John Cornelius Hodges",
#=>     tracks: #Ecto.Association.NotLoaded<association
#=>       :tracks is not loaded>,
#=>     updated_at: ~N[2018-03-23 14:02:28]
#=>   }
#=> }}
```

Now we can get a good look at that last value. The keys in the map correspond to our named Multi functions that have already been run. In this example, we just had the one :artist update so that's all this map contains. The value of the item is the result of the operation. Here we can see that our "Johnny Hodges" record was updated to "John Cornelius Hodges" as we expected. But because the Multi failed (thanks to the addition of our bad_genre operation), the database rolled back the change. We can confirm that by looking at the database again:

```
Repo.get_by(Artist, name: "John Cornelius Hodges")
#=> nil
```

We get no records back when we search for "John Cornelius Hodges," which confirms that our update was indeed rolled back.

Optimizing Multi with Changesets

One important consideration with Multi is that the transaction call works with unhandled errors the same way as it does with functions: they're bubbled up to the function that called the transaction. Consider this example:

```
multi =
  Multi.new
  |> Multi.insert(:artist, %Artist{})
    Repo.transaction(multi)
    #=> ** (Postgrex.Error) ERROR 23502 (not_null_violation): null value
    #=>  in column "name" violates not-null constraint
```

Instead of passing a changeset to insert we passed in an empty Artist struct. Our database requires that all records in artists have a non-null name field, so the insert operation fails. This results in transaction raising an error, rather than returning the nicely arranged tuple we saw in the last example.

Given this behavior, it's best to use changesets with Multi whenever possible. Creating changesets with validations will help Ecto catch errors within the bounds of your Elixir code before they hit the database. Of course, you always need to consider that unhandled errors can happen, and you'll need to design your code to respond to those errors in a way that minimizes impact to your users. But you can reduce the occurrences of those kinds of errors by fortifying your changesets as much as possible.

Executing Non-Database Operations with Multi

Based on what we've seen of Multi so far, it might appear that executing transaction with functions has one clear advantage: functions allow you to run any Elixir code within the transaction. Recall our earlier example of updating a search engine within a transaction call. Fortunately, Multi offers this functionality as well. The run function allows you to add any named or anonymous function to be run as part of the Multi. Here's how we might add the search engine update logic we talked about earlier in this chapter:

```
priv/examples/transactions_07.exs
artist = %Artist{name: "Toshiko Akiyoshi"}
multi =
  Multi.new()
  |> Multi.insert(:artist, artist)
  |> Multi.insert(:log, Log.changeset_for_insert(artist))
  |> Multi.run(:search, fn _repo, changes ->
    SearchEngine.update(changes[:artist])
  end)
Repo.transaction(multi)
```

In this example, we used an anonymous function for the run operation. The function accepts two arguments, our current Repo and a map of the changes made in the Multi so far. We need the Artist record that we inserted, so we grab the :artist item from the changes map. Ecto expects our function to return {:ok, value} if the function succeeded or {:error, value} if it failed. In that case, value can be any value of our choosing.

For more flexibility, we can use Multi.run/5, which lets us specify the module, the function, and a list of additional arguments separately:

```
multi =
  Multi.new()
  |> Multi.insert(:artist, artist)
  |> Multi.insert(:log, Log.changeset_for_insert(artist))
  |> Multi.run(:search, SearchEngine, :update, ["extra argument"])
```

With this form of run, Ecto will still pass in the Repo and the list of changes to the specified function—these will be the first arguments passed to the function, with the arguments you specify immediately following. The last line in the preceding code will result in SearchEngine.update being called like this: SearchEngine.update(repo, changes, "extra argument").

The run function gives you the flexibility to execute any Elixir code as part of your transaction. This is useful for non-database operations, but it's also useful for database operations that Multi does not directly support. For example, there is no Multi.all function to mirror the Repo.all function. If you need to run a query within an operation, you could call Repo.all within a function called by run.

Introspection with Multi

Given that Multi is a data structure, it can sometimes be useful to examine its contents. The Ecto team discourages inspecting or manipulating the internals of a Multi struct directly, as the exact structure is subject to change. But you can use the to_list function to see the all of the operations currently queued within a Multi:

```
multi =
  Multi.new()
  |> Multi.insert(:artist, artist)
  |> Multi.insert(:log, Log.changeset_for_insert(artist))
  |> Multi.run(:search, SearchEngine, :update, ["extra argument"])
Multi.to_list(multi)
#=> [
#=>   artist: {:insert,
#=>     #Ecto.Changeset<action: :insert, changes: %{}, errors: [],
#=>      data: #MusicDB.Artist<>, valid?: true>, []},
#=>   log: {:insert,
#=>     #Ecto.Changeset<action: :insert, changes: %{}, errors: [],
#=>      data: #MusicDB.Log<>, valid?: true>, []},
#=>   search: {:run, {SearchEngine, :update, ["extra argument"]}}
#=> ]
```

This comes in handy for testing. It allows you to verify that any code that generates a Multi is producing the right data structure, without actually having to run it against the database. This can simplify your test considerably, as you don't have to worry about having the database in the correct state before you run the test. Your test suite will also run considerably faster if you can avoid unnecessary round-trips to the database.

Wrapping Up

Ecto has excellent support for database transactions via the Repo.transaction function. The last section covered some of the ways that using Ecto.Multi is preferable to using functions, but cases definitely exist where calling transaction with a function works well.

If you're only running a small number of operations and you don't need to take different action depending on which operation succeeds or fails, using a function is a good option. For all other cases, you should consider Ecto.Multi. It has a lot more flexibility, and the code needed to respond to different types of errors will be much cleaner and easier to follow.

We've almost completed our tour of Ecto. We've looked at how to run queries, make changes, map records to structs, and group operations together. Along the way, we've worked through numerous examples based on the dataset included with the MusicDB sample app. For our last stop, we'll take a look at how that dataset got created in the first place. The Ecto.Migration module provides tools to set up your database tables from within your Elixir code, and make changes to them over the life of your application. With this last piece of the puzzle, you'll be ready to create your own app and put your Ecto knowledge to work.

## CHAPTER 6

Making Changes to Your Database

For this last stop on our tour of Ecto, we are going back to the beginning.

In previous chapters, we've queried, updated, deleted, and sometimes mangled the dataset that came with our MusicDB app. Now we're going to take a look at how those tables got created in the first place.

Ecto uses *migrations* to create and alter tables in your database. A migration is a set of commands, created in Elixir, that contains the instructions for the changes you want to make. Ecto provides mix tasks to help you create, run and even roll back your migrations.

In this chapter, we'll look at the Ecto.Migration module and work with the tools it provides to help you create and maintain the structure of your database throughout the lifetime of your app.

Introducing Migrations

Migrations solve an age-old problem: keeping the structure of the database in sync between production systems, staging systems, and the local systems running on each developer's computer. This used to be a manual process and it was prone to error. A hot fix made on a production system might not propagate back to the developer's systems, leading to errors that were hard to track down. Migrations help automate this process and provide a consistent framework for making changes across all the systems in your organization.

When adding a new feature that requires changes to the database, you write a migration: a single Elixir module that can execute the changes you want to make. You store that migration in source control along with the rest of your code. When you run the migration on a particular database instance, Ecto makes the changes specified in your migration to that database, and keeps track of which migrations have already been run.

When it comes time to deploy your app to another system, you tell Ecto to run migrations for this system. It checks to see which of the migrations in your code have already been run, and executes any newly added migrations. Because Ecto keeps track of which migrations have already been run, everyone can stay in sync. A new developer coming on the project for the first time would end up running all of the migrations at once the first time they set up the project.

Your migrations use the Ecto.Migration API to create and modify database tables using Elixir code. This allows your migrations to be database-independent: the same migrations can be used with any database that Ecto supports.

We'll work through a number of different examples in the following sections of this chapter, but if you're curious, you can take a sneak peek at the migrations we used in the MusicDB app by looking at the files in the priv/repo/migrations directory. It's OK if they don't make sense to you right away—hopefully by the end of this chapter, they will.

Your First Migration

To get a feel for how to write migrations, we're going to add a new table to our MusicDB project.

We've been using the tracks table to keep track of recordings of songs that have appeared on specific albums. But many artists record songs that they did not write themselves, and certain songs appear on more than one album. For example, in our current dataset, the song "Freddie Freeloader" appears on two different albums. We'll create a compositions table to track the metadata of the songs that appear in our dataset, and later link them to specific tracks records.

The easiest way to create a new migration is to use the mix task that Ecto provides: mix ecto.gen.migration. This task has one required argument: the name of the migration you want to create. Ecto will use this name in the migration module it will create for you. It's best to make this name as descriptive as possible so that future developers (or future you) can understand what the migrations do just by looking at the names. We're going to create a new compositions table so we'll call it add_compositions_table.

You can specify the name using snake case:

```
mix ecto.gen.migration add_compositions_table
```

or Pascal case:

```
mix ecto.gen.migration AddCompositionsTable
```

Either way, you'll get the same result. Pick either of these commands, and run it in a terminal window. You should see something like this:

```
* creating priv/repo/migrations
* creating priv/repo/migrations/20180410132202_add_compositions_table.exs
```

By default, Ecto puts all the migrations it generates into priv/[YOUR_REPO]/migrations. We named our repo Repo so Ecto uses priv/repo/migrations. Our project only has one repo, so Ecto could infer where to put the migration. If we were using multiple repos, we'd need to specify which one we want to apply the migration to with the -r option:

```
mix ecto.gen.migration AddCompositionsTable -r MusicDB.Repo
```

You may have noticed Ecto added a timestamp to the filename it generated:

```
* creating priv/repo/migrations/20180410132202_add_compositions_table.exs
```

This timestamp serves two purposes. First, it acts as a unique ID that Ecto uses to keep track of which migrations have been run. Second, it helps ensure that migrations are run in the correct order. In many cases, you'll write migrations that make changes to existing tables. It's important that the migrations that generate those tables are run before the ones that alter them.

Let's take a look at the generated file and see what Ecto created for us. Open up the file in your text editor and you should see something like this:

```elixir
defmodule MusicDB.Repo.Migrations.AddCompositionsTable do
  use Ecto.Migration

  def change do

  end
end
```

We've got a standard Elixir module, with a use statement, as we've seen before. There's also an empty change function. This is the function that Ecto will call when running the migration, so this is where we'll put our code to create the new table. Let's do that now.

We'll start with just three fields: a string to represent the title of the composition, an integer for year it was composed, and a foreign key to the artists table to indicate the composer of the song:

```
priv/examples/migrations_01.exs
defmodule MusicDB.Repo.Migrations.AddCompositionsTable do
  use Ecto.Migration

  def change do
    create table("compositions") do
      add :title, :string, null: false
      add :year, :integer, null: false
      add :artist_id, references("artists"), null: false
      timestamps()
    end
  end
end
```

We create a new table by calling the create function. The table function creates a new Ecto.Migration.Table struct with the name we provide ("compositions" in this case).

We then create a do/end block that specifies the columns of our new table using the add function. In each call to add we specify the name of the column and the type.

You have two options when specifying the type. You can use the Ecto types we learned about in Chapter 3, Connecting Your Tables to Elixir Structs with Schemas, on page 41, and Ecto will translate those into the corresponding database-specific types. Or, you can provide the actual database type yourself, provided that it's one that Ecto knows about.

For example, Ecto translates the :string type to character varying(255) in PostgreSQL. If you were creating a column that needed to handle long strings of text, you might define the column using :text. Ecto will still use Elixir's String type for these values in your Elixir code, but using :text ensures that the database column will be able to hold as much text as you need.

For the artist_id column, we didn't provide an atom for the type, and instead called the references function. This tells Ecto that we'd like artist_id to be a foreign key for the artists table. As we'll see in a moment, this will cause Ecto to do a little extra work for us when setting up the table in the database.

We've added the null: false option to our columns because we do not want any of them to allow null as a value. We will most likely add validations to our changesets to prevent this as well, but it's important to have the rules enforced at the database level, just to be absolutely sure you don't end up with values you don't want.

The add function will also accept a default: option that allows you to provide a fallback value if the user doesn't provide one. There's no sensible default we could provide for these columns, so we've omitted that option here.

timestamps is a convenience function that adds two datetime columns: inserted_at and updated_at. As we saw in Chapter 3, Connecting Your Tables to Elixir Structs with Schemas, on page 41, Ecto will provide values for these columns automatically when you insert or update records using schemas.

By default, Ecto uses Elixir's NaiveDateTime and does not preserve microsecond information (it will discard it when running Changeset.cast and raise an error if you try to set the value in a schema struct). If you need time zones or microseconds in your timestamps, you can change the default timestamp type. We'll show you how to do that in Changing Timestamps, on page 117.

Running Migrations

Now that we've got our first migration written, let's try running it and see what it does. Ecto provides a mix task to do this, so jump back out to the command line, and run mix ecto.migrate. You should see something like this:

```
06:57:27.065 [info]  == Running
MusicDB.Repo.Migrations.AddCompositionsTable.change/0 forward
06:57:27.065 [info]  create table compositions
06:57:27.069 [info]  == Migrated in 0.0s
```

This tells us that the migration was successful, and Ecto added our new table.

Let's take a peek at our database and see what it did.

We're going to open our database console so we can examine the tables directly. The following examples will show the steps for working with PostgreSQL—if you're using MySQL, you'll need to run the equivalent commands.

You can open up a PostgreSQL console with the psql command:

```
$ psql music_db
psql (10.3)
Type "help" for help.

music_db=#
```

From here we can use the \dt command to see a list of tables:

```
music_db=# \dt
               List of relations
 Schema |       Name        | Type  | Owner
--------+-------------------+-------+-------
 public | albums            | table | darin
 public | albums_genres     | table | darin
 public | artists           | table | darin
 public | compositions      | table | darin
 public | genres            | table | darin
 public | logs              | table | darin
 public | schema_migrations | table | darin
 public | tracks            | table | darin
(8 rows)
```

And there in the middle we can see our new compositions table. Let's look at the details of that table using the \d command:

```
music_db=# \d compositions
   Column   |            Type             | Collation | Nullable
------------+-----------------------------+-----------+----------
 id         | bigint                      |           | not null
 title      | character varying(255)      |           |
 year       | integer                     |           |
 artist_id  | bigint                      |           |
 inserted_at | timestamp without time zone |          | not null
 updated_at | timestamp without time zone |           | not null
Indexes:
    "compositions_pkey" PRIMARY KEY, btree (id)
Foreign-key constraints:
    "compositions_artist_id_fkey" FOREIGN KEY (artist_id)
    REFERENCES artists(id)
```

We've truncated some of the output so it will fit in the book, but this shows most of what you need to see. The first row comes as a surprise: there's an id column, and the Indexes section tells us that id is the primary key. We didn't put this in our migration, so what's it doing here?

Ecto added this column for us. It will always create a primary key column called id unless you tell it not to. This is handy because most of the time you will need a column like this, and having a primary key named id is a common convention. However, it's possible to disable this behavior if you need to—we'll see how to do that later in this chapter.

The rest of the columns are what we expect: we have the title, year, and artist_id columns we created using the add function. For artist_id Ecto added a foreign key constraint (thanks to our addition of the references call).

The timestamps function in our migration gave us the inserted_at and updated_at columns we see here. Notice that these are set to the timestamp without time zone type. Ecto will use this type by default (which maps to the NaiveDateTime type in Elixir), but you can change this behavior as well.

While we're in the console, let's take a look at another table. You may have noticed schema_migrations in the list of tables when we ran the \dt command earlier—that's not one that we've used in any of the previous chapters. This table is created and maintained by Ecto—it's where it keeps track of the migrations that it has already run. It's a regular table just like our other ones, so we can look at it with a select statement:

```
music_db=# select * from schema_migrations;
     version     |         inserted_at
-----------------+----------------------------
 20180308131742  | 2018-04-11 13:57:09.221876
 20180308132308  | 2018-04-11 13:57:09.244394
 20180308134145  | 2018-04-11 13:57:09.261668
 20180308134445  | 2018-04-11 13:57:09.280168
 20180308134653  | 2018-04-11 13:57:09.299608
 20180313132703  | 2018-04-11 13:57:09.316839
 20180410134047  | 2018-04-11 13:57:27.077176
(7 rows)
```

The version column contains the timestamps of the migrations that have been successfully run (these are the timestamps that Ecto adds to migration file-names). When we run mix ecto.migrate, Ecto compares the list of migrations in our codebase to the list of versions in this table. It then runs, in order, any migrations that aren't in this table, and adds a new record if the migration completes.

Rolling Back Migrations

Sometimes you want to undo the changes you made in a migration. This happens frequently in development—you'll often change your mind about what your table should look like so it's common to create a migration, roll it back, make some changes and run it again. But it can also happen when your app is in production as well, when you have one of those dreaded "oops" moments.

Ecto provides the ecto.rollback mix task to roll back one or more migrations. Let's try that out now:

```
$ mix ecto.rollback
06:17:40.823 [info]  == Running
MusicDB.Repo.Migrations.AddCompositionsTable.change/0 backward

06:17:40.824 [info]  drop table compositions

06:17:40.831 [info]  == Migrated in 0.0s
```

The output tells us that our most recent migration was rolled back: instead of creating a new table, we dropped it. In this case, Ecto was able to infer the rollback behavior of the change function in our migration. It saw that we were creating a table, so to roll it back, it determined that it should drop the table. This will work for many, if not most, of the changes you'll make with migrations. Ecto will complain loudly if it encounters anything it can't figure out. In those cases, you'll have to be explicit about what the rollback behavior should be. We'll look at some examples of that later in the chapter.

When developing new migrations, it's a good idea to make sure you can roll them back. Part of testing a migration is making sure it runs and rolls back successfully, always leaving the database in a stable state. You don't want to be trying this out for the first time while you're dealing with a production emergency.

By default, mix ecto.migrate will run all the migrations that haven't been run yet, and mix ecto.rollback will roll back only the most recent migration. But both of these commands accept options that change this behavior. For example:

```
mix ecto.migrate -n 3
```

will run the first three pending migrations, and

```
mix ecto.rollback -n 3
```

will roll back the three most recent migrations. Similarly:

```
mix ecto.migrate -v 20080906120000
```

will run all of the pending migrations up to and including the given version number, and

```
mix ecto.rollback -v 20080906120000
```

will roll back all of the most recent migrations down to and including the version.

To see all of the options available in these commands, run mix help ecto.migrate and mix help ecto.rollback.

Adding Indexes

Our table is looking good so far, but there's a looming problem that will start to bite us before too long. We didn't add any indexes, which will slow down our queries substantially. Let's fix that now.

Edit a Migration or Create a New One?

This change brings up an interesting question: should we generate a new migration to add these indexes, or should we just edit the migration that we already made?

As a general rule, it's OK to edit an existing migration *provided that you haven't already committed your migration to source control*. Once your migration is available to other developers on your team, you shouldn't make any edits to it—you should instead create a new migration with the changes you want to make.

The reason is a practical one. Once a migration is committed, you can't be certain that other developers haven't already pulled it down and run it on their machine. Ecto can't detect changes to a migration that's already been run, so your teammates won't be able to apply your new changes just by running mix ecto.migrate. You would need to go to them directly and tell them to roll back that migration, pull down your changes, and run the migration again. (This is usually not a pleasant conversation—trust us on this one.) If you instead create a new migration, they just need to sync their codebase, run the new migration, and they're back on track.

Changing an Existing Table

To get more practice generating migrations, let's assume that we've already committed our previous migration, so we'll create a new one to add our indexes. We imagine that we'll often want to query this table by title and year so we're going to add indexes for those two columns.

First, go back out to the command line and run mix ecto.gen.migration as we did before:

```
$ mix ecto.gen.migration add_indexes_to_compositions
* creating priv/repo/migrations
* creating
  priv/repo/migrations/20180413123728_add_indexes_to_compositions.exs
```

Now open the new file in your text editor, and edit it so it looks like this:

```
priv/examples/migrations_02.exs
defmodule MusicDB.Repo.Migrations.AddIndexesToCompositions do
  use Ecto.Migration

  def change do
    create index("compositions", :title)
    create index("compositions", :year)
  end
end
```

We use create as we did in our last migration, but instead of calling table we call index and provide the table and column names for the index. If you need an index that combines multiple columns, you can provide a list of column names.

```
# create an index on the title and year columns together
create index("compositions", [:title, :year])
```

Now we can jump back out to the command line and try running and rolling back our migration:

```
$ mix ecto.migrate

06:00:23.187 [info]  ==
Running MusicDB.Repo.Migrations.AddIndexesToCompositions.change/0 forward

06:00:23.187 [info]  create index compositions_title_index

06:00:23.190 [info]  create index compositions_year_index

06:00:23.193 [info]  == Migrated in 0.0s

$ mix ecto.rollback

06:00:30.298 [info]  ==
Running MusicDB.Repo.Migrations.AddIndexesToCompositions.change/0 backward

06:00:30.298 [info]  drop index compositions_year_index

06:00:30.299 [info]  drop index compositions_title_index

06:00:30.300 [info]  == Migrated in 0.0s
```

The drop index lines that appear in the output assure us that Ecto has once again inferred how to roll back our migration for us.

Adding Options to an Index

The index function supports several options that control the behavior of the index.

One important one is unique. When set to true, the database will prevent creating two records with the same value for this column. We used this for the name column of the genres table to make sure that we don't end up with duplicate genre names:

priv/examples/migrations_02.exs
```
create index("genres", :name, unique: true)
```

This option is used often enough that Ecto provides the unique_index function as a shortcut. You add the same index by writing this instead:

```
create unique_index("genres", :name)
```

Database indexes must have a name, and Ecto provides one for you by default by combining the table and column names of the index ("compositions_year_index," for example). Most of the time this convention works fine, but if you're creating a multi-column index and some of the column names are long, it's possible that the name Ecto generates will be longer than your database allows. If that happens, you can use the name option to provide a name the database can use:

```
create index("compositions", :title, name: "title_index")
```

Other options support things like the index type, partial indexes, and so on. For more details, see the Ecto docs.[1]

Changing Data and Table Structure Together

Our new compositions table is working better now that we've added some indexes, but as we start adding data, we discover another problem. Our current structure only allows us to associate one composer with each record, and some songs have more than one composer. As we think about it further, we realize that many songs have separate composers and lyricists, and we might want to capture that info as well.

This sounds like a job for a many-to-many relationship between compositions and artists: a composition can have many artists, and an artist can contribute to many songs. As we discussed in Chapter 3, Connecting Your Tables to Elixir Structs with Schemas, on page 41 we'll need a new join table between compositions and artists. In addition to the foreign keys for these two tables, we'll also include a role column so we can specify the relationship as "composer" or "lyricist." Let's set that up now.

First, we'll generate a new migration:

```
$ mix ecto.gen.migration add_composition_artists_table
* creating priv/repo/migrations
* creating
  priv/repo/migrations/20180413134804_add_composition_artists_table.exs
```

---

1. https://hexdocs.pm/ecto_sql/Ecto.Migration.html#index/3

Next, we'll add the code to create our new table. And we won't forget the indexes this time!

```
priv/examples/migrations_03.exs
defmodule MusicDB.Repo.Migrations.AddCompositionArtistsTable do
  use Ecto.Migration

  def change do
    create table("compositions_artists") do
      add :composition_id, references("compositions"), null: false
      add :artist_id, references("artists"), null: false
      add :role, :string, null: false
    end

    create index("compositions_artists", :composition_id)
    create index("compositions_artists", :artist_id)
  end
end
```

That handles setting up the new table. Now we need to think about how we're going to alter the data that's already in the compositions table. We know that we're going to remove the artist_id column, as that data is now going to live in our new table, but we don't want to lose the values in that column. We want to move them into the new table.

In a situation like this, you can use migrations not only to change database structure, but also to move data around when you need to. In our case, we want to take the id and artist_id values from each record in compositions and use them to insert a new record into compositions_artists. We had only been keeping track of composers so far, so we'll set role to "composer" for each of the new records.

We haven't changed our schemas to work with our new tables, so we can use a schema-less query and insert_all to do the work we need:

```
def change do
  #...

  from(c in "compositions", select: [:id, :artist_id])
  |> Repo.all()
  |> Enum.each(fn row ->
    Repo.insert_all("compositions_artists", [
      [composition_id: row.id, artist_id: row.artist_id, role: "composer"]
    ])
  end)
end
```

To keep this example simpler, we're assuming that we don't have a huge number of records in compositions and running them all through Enum.each/2 won't create a problem. For large record sets, you'd want to take a different approach—we'll talk about that in Chapter 17, Tuning for Performance, on page 201.

Once we've moved the old data into the new table, we can safely remove the artist_id column from the compositions table. We use the alter function to make changes to table columns:

```
def change do
  #...

  alter table("compositions") do
    remove :artist_id
  end
end
```

Everything looks really good, but we're not quite done. If we tried to run the migration right now, we'd get an error like this:

```
** (Postgrex.Error) ERROR 42P01 (undefined_table):
  relation "compositions_artists" does not exist
```

That's a confusing error. Of course the table doesn't exist—we're trying to create it now. This seems like an unfair complaint.

The problem has to do with the way Ecto runs migrations. Instead of running each of the operations one at a time, it creates a queue of operations that it sends to the database all at once. In that moment, our insert into compositions_artists isn't a viable statement because that table isn't in the database yet.

Fortunately, there's a workaround. The flush function tells Ecto to execute the currently queued operations—any code that comes after the flush call can assume that all the prior changes have been run. For our migration, we need to add the flush right before we start trying to change the data:

```
def change do
  #...

  create(index("compositions_artists", :composition_id))
  create(index("compositions_artists", :artist_id))

  flush()

  from(c in "compositions", select: [:id, :artist_id])
  |> Repo.all()

  #...

end
```

When you're writing migrations that involve data changes as well as structural changes, you'll often need flush so that you can act on the results of previous parts of the migration. If you get an error saying that the database can't find something you think should be there, double-check that you're calling flush in the right places.

Here is our migration in full. Note the addition of import Ecto.Query and alias MusicDB.Repo at the top:

```elixir
defmodule MusicDB.Repo.Migrations.AddCompositionsArtistsTable do
  use Ecto.Migration
  import Ecto.Query
  alias MusicDB.Repo

  def change do
    create table("compositions_artists") do
      add(:composition_id, references("compositions"), null: false)
      add(:artist_id, references("artists"), null: false)
      add(:role, :string, null: false)
    end

    create(index("compositions_artists", :composition_id))
    create(index("compositions_artists", :artist_id))

    flush()

    from(c in "compositions", select: [:id, :artist_id])
    |> Repo.all()
    |> Enum.each(fn row ->
      Repo.insert_all("compositions_artists", [
        [composition_id: row.id, artist_id: row.artist_id, role: "composer"]
      ])
    end)

    alter table("compositions") do
      remove :artist_id
    end
  end
end
```

Now, it's ready to run. It'll create the new table, and move the data all at once.

Specifying Up and Down Operations

In the last section, we created a migration that altered data as well as structure, but we left out an important step. In its current form, this migration can't be rolled back.

Ecto can't reverse the removal of a column, because it wouldn't know what type it should be restored back to. And we certainly can't expect Ecto to figure out how to reverse the data transformation we did between compositions and compositions_artists. We need to specify the rollback instructions ourselves.

In cases like these, you write the migration differently. Instead of providing a single change function, you write an up function and a down function, to handle the migration going forward and rolling back, respectively. Let's rewrite the migration so it can be rolled back.

Right now, our change function has all the logic we need for going forward. We just need to rename the function from change to up. But we still need to write the down function.

Here's how we might do it:

```
priv/examples/migrations_04.exs
def down do
  alter table("compositions") do
    add :artist_id, references("artists")
  end

  flush()

  from(ca in "compositions_artists", where: ca.role == "composer",
      select: [:composition_id, :artist_id])
  |> Repo.all()
  |> Enum.each(fn row ->
    Repo.update_all(
      from(c in "compositions", where: c.id == ^row.composition_id),
      set: [artist_id: row.artist_id]
    )
  end)

  drop table("compositions_artists")
end
```

First, we put artist_id back into the compositions table. Then we call flush so that the new column is available for us to move data into it.

Now we need to move the artist_id from compositions_artists back into the compositions table. If we've added any new records where there's more than one artist associated with a composition, we're going to lose some of that data—unfortunately, we have no choice there. We get all the compositions_artists records with the role of composer, then update the associated compositions record with the artist_id. If any composition had more than one composer associated with it, the last one will win. We can't do much about that, except hope that we never have to roll this migration back.

Finally, we drop the compositions_artists table, and we're back to where we were.

Changing Default Behaviors

Ecto's migrations follow a number of conventions that have proven to work well over time. In most cases, it's easiest to follow those conventions. They usually require less code and they can reduce ramp-up time for new developers joining the project—it's always helpful if a new project looks a lot like your last one. But sometimes Ecto's conventions won't fit your project, and you need to structure things differently. Fortunately, Ecto offers a number of escape hatches that allow you to craft your migrations as needed. In this section, we'll look at a number of different ways you can customize migration behavior.

Setting Primary and Foreign Key Names

Earlier in this chapter, we saw how Ecto automatically creates a primary key called id with type :bigserial when you create a new table. If you'd like Ecto to use a different name and/or type when creating primary keys, you can set this as a global configuration option in your Repo config in config/config.exs (we looked at some of these configuration settings in Chapter 1, Getting Started with Repo, on page 3). Here's how you could use code instead of id as the column name, and :string as the type:

```
config :music_db, MusicDB.Repo,
  migration_primary_key: [id: :code, type: :string]
```

Making this change affects the default behavior whenever you create a new table with Ecto. But you can change the behavior on a per-table basis as well. Anytime you don't want Ecto to create a primary key for you, add the primary_key: false option when creating the table:

```
priv/examples/migrations_05.exs
create table("compositions", primary_key: false) do
  add :title, :string, null: false
  #...
end
```

You could then add a primary key to the table manually when calling add:

```
create table("compositions", primary_key: false) do
  add :code, :string, primary_key: true
  #...
end
```

This is useful when you're using Ecto to connect to legacy databases that weren't created with Ecto's naming conventions in mind.

When creating foreign keys with the references function, Ecto again assumes that the primary key of the referenced table is called id and is a :bigserial. But you can pass options to references to specify something different:

```
create table("compositions_artists") do
  add :composition_id, references("compositions",
    column: "code", type: "string")
  #...
end
```

As a general rule, it's good to follow Ecto's conventions whenever you can. But if you can't, you can have several options for changing the way Ecto references keys.

Changing Timestamps

Earlier we saw how the timestamps method automatically adds inserted_at and updated_at columns to your tables. By default, these will always use Elixir's NaiveDateTime type, but you can change this globally in your Repo config. Here's how you could change it to use a UTC timestamp:

```
config :music_db, MusicDB.Repo, migration_timestamps: [type: :utc_datetime]
```

The :time, :naive_datetime, and :utc_datetime types don't allow you to save microsecond information in your timestamps. If you need microseconds, you can use the more precise counterparts: :time_usec, :naive_datetime_usec, or :utc_datetime_usec.

Making this change in the Repo config will affect any timestamps call you make in any of your migrations, but you can customize this behavior at the table level as well. The timestamps function lets you specify the datetime type you'd like to use, and even lets you change the column names.

This will add the two timestamps columns to compositions, but they'll be named created_at and changed_at instead of inserted_at and updated_at, and they'll use UTC timestamps:

priv/examples/migrations_05.exs
```
create table("compositions") do
  timestamps(inserted_at: :created_at, updated_at: :changed_at,
    type: :utc_datetime)
  #...
end
```

Note if you're using schemas, changing the timestamp type in the migration or the Repo config isn't enough to guarantee your timestamps will be stored correctly. You'll also need to set the type in the Ecto.Schema.timestamps/1 call when you define the Schema. See the documentation[2] for more details.

You can also set the inserted_at or updated_at options to false if you don't want to include that column. This will add inserted_at, but not updated_at:

```
create table("compositions") do
  timestamps updated_at: false
  #...
end
```

_____

2.   https://hexdocs.pm/ecto/Ecto.Schema.html#timestamps/1

You have quite a lot of options when setting up Ecto's timestamps, but it's usually best to pick one approach and stick with it throughout your database, if you can.

Running Migrations Outside of a Transaction

By default, migrations are run within a database transaction. This is a good thing: if any part of your migration has an error, you can be assured that the database will be restored back to the way it was. But there may be times when you won't want to do it this way. In those cases, you can disable the transactional behavior by setting the module attribute @disable_ddl_transaction to true:

```
priv/examples/migrations_05.exs
defmodule MusicDB.Repo.Migrations.AddCompositionsIndex do
  use Ecto.Migration
  @disable_ddl_transaction true

  def change do
    #...
  end
end
```

One situation where you need to do this is when changing indexes concurrently. Databases usually prevent tables from accepting new writes while adding or dropping indexes, but PostgreSQL has an option that removes this limitation. This is useful if you need to alter an index on a large table, and don't want it unavailable for writes during the process.

You can take advantage of this feature by setting the concurrently option to true while creating the index, but you must run the migration outside of a transaction by settings @disable_ddl_transaction to true.

For creating indexes concurrently, there's one more change we need to make. We need to set the migration_lock configuration option for our Repo to nil. By default, Ecto will lock the schema_migrations table when running migrations. This lets multiple nodes run migrations, but only allows one of them to succeed. Normally, that's a good thing, but it interferes with our ability to create the index concurrently. So we need to disable the lock in our Repo configuration:

```
config :music_db, MusicDB.Repo, migration_lock: nil
```

Once that's done, our migration will look like this:

```
defmodule MusicDB.Repo.Migrations.AddCompositionsIndex do
  use Ecto.Migration
  @disable_ddl_transaction true

  def change do
    create index("compositions", :title, concurrently: true)
  end
end
```

If you omit setting @disable_ddl_transaction for this change, you will get an error like this:

```
** (Postgrex.Error) ERROR 25001 (active_sql_transaction):
CREATE INDEX CONCURRENTLY cannot run inside a transaction block
```

Running migrations without a transaction is useful in a few situations, but you'll want to do this carefully. It could be difficult to restore your database if something goes wrong. If you need to use this option, keep the migration as small as possible. Try to restrict the migration to only those operations that must be run outside a transaction. Everything else should be run in a separate transactional migration. This will help reduce the damage if something goes awry.

Wrapping Up

Ecto's migrations help you manage the structure of your database throughout the lifetime of your application. We covered the main features of migrations in this chapter, but as always, it's good to review the official documentation to see all of the supported features. You may also want to read through the migrations that came with the MusicDB codebase to see more real-life examples.

This wraps up our tour of the main Ecto modules. You should now have a solid understanding of the basics, and you're ready to look at some more advanced topics in Part II. Feel free to skip around and focus on the chapters that are most interesting to you. Each chapter in Part II stands on its own and can be read in any order.

Part II

Ecto Applied

With the knowledge acquired in Part I, we'll look at some more advanced use cases that often come up with Ecto and database programming in general. We'll cover such topics as performance tuning, speeding up your tests with sandboxes, integrating with Phoenix, and the like. Each chapter is distinct, so feel free to jump directly into the topics you're most interested in, and look at the others later on.

## CHAPTER 7

Adding Ecto to an Elixir Application Without Phoenix

We hope that by now, you're so enthralled with Ecto that you want to add it to all your projects right away (we can dream, can't we?). Adding Ecto to a project isn't too difficult, but it does require a few more steps beyond just adding the hex package to your list of dependencies.

Most of the time, you won't need to worry about this. Phoenix projects, for example, have Ecto included in their initial setup, and the music app we were playing with in Part I came with Ecto included as well. But there may be times when you'll need to add Ecto to a project yourself. This chapter will show you how to do that, by walking you through the following steps:

- Creating a new project
- Adding Ecto and its dependencies
- Creating and configuring your Repo module
- Adding Ecto to the supervision tree
- Starting the app

Open up a new terminal window, and let's get started!

Creating a New Project

The first step is to create a new Elixir application with the mix tool. A new app needs a lot of boilerplate, but mix new does all the heavy lifting for us:

```
> mix new my_app --sup
* creating README.md
* creating .gitignore
* creating mix.exs
* creating config
```

```
* creating config/config.exs
* creating lib
* creating lib/my_app.ex
* creating lib/my_app/application.ex
* creating test
* creating test/test_helper.exs
* creating test/my_app_test.exs

Your Mix project was created successfully.
You can use "mix" to compile it, test it, and more:

    cd my_app
    mix test

Run "mix help" for more commands.
```

Note that we added the --sup flag to mix new. This is because Ecto does all of its work in separate OTP processes. It needs to be part of a supervision tree to make sure that it starts up correctly, and is restarted if a process fails.

What is a supervision tree?

One of the many benefits of working with Elixir is having access to OTP (Open Telecom Platform), provided by the underlying Erlang runtime. OTP allows you to organize your programs into lightweight independent execution units called *processes*. You can use *supervisors* to observe processes and restart them if they fail. It's also possible to have supervisors observing other supervisors, and as programs increase in complexity, there can many groups of processes and supervisors all working together at the same time. We refer to this structure as a *supervision tree*, because it has a single starting point in your application, and fans out from there.

Many third-party libraries, including Ecto, manage their own supervision trees so it's likely that you've had them in your applications, whether you've been aware of them or not. OTP is a big topic, certainly more than we can cover here, but if you'd like to read more, a good starting point is the *Mix and OTP Guide* on the Elixir website.[1]

If you want to add Ecto to an application that was not generated with the --sup flag, you'll have a little extra configuration to do—we'll come back to that in a bit.

---

1.   https://elixir-lang.org/getting-started/mix-otp/introduction-to-mix.html

Adding Ecto's Dependencies

The next step is to add the packages that Ecto needs to run. Open the mix.exs file and look for the deps/0 function. It should look something like this:

```
defp deps do
  [
    # {:dep_from_hexpm, "~> 0.3.0"},
    # {:dep_from_git, git: "https://github.com/elixir-lang/my_dep.git",
    #   tag: "0.1.0"}
  ]
end
```

Replace the commented-out code with the following:

priv/examples/adding_ecto.exs
```
defp deps do
  [
    {:postgrex, ">= 0.0.0"},
    {:ecto_sql, "~> 3.0"}
  ]
end
```

Postgrex is the driver Ecto uses to communicate with the PostgreSQL database. Ecto also supports MySQL and MariaDB out of the box with the mariaex adapter—you just need to replace {:postgrex, ">= 0.0.0"} with {:mariaex, ">= 0.0.0"} (this adapter works for both MySQL and MariaDB). As of this writing, a new driver called myxql is in development, and should be ready when Ecto 3.1 is released. If you're using Ecto 3.1 or later, you can use the new driver by replacing mariaex with myxql in your list of dependencies.

For all these drivers, we use the >= 0.0.0 version requirement to let Ecto decide which versions it wants; in this case we don't have a specific requirement.

Creating Your Repo Module

Next we need to create our app's repository module. We went through this process in detail in Chapter 1, Getting Started with Repo, on page 3 but we'll run through it again here.

Open a new file called lib/my_app/repo.ex and add the following:

```
defmodule MyApp.Repo do
  use Ecto.Repo,
    otp_app: :my_app,
    adapter: Ecto.Adapters.Postgres
end
```

The use Ecto.Repo directive will make our module a bona fide Ecto repository—all of Ecto's repository functions will be defined and made available on this module. For more details on how this works, see The Repo Module, on page 10.

The otp_app: :my_app option tells Ecto where to find the repository configuration. So far, our project only has the my_app application, so we're using that value here. If we had multiple applications in this project, you could store the Repo configuration in any one of them, and provide the name of that application rather than :my_app.

We also need to set the adapter: option so Ecto knows which database we want to use. In this case we are using PostgreSQL so we'll use Ecto.Adapters.Postgres as the adapter. It can be changed to Ecto.Adapters.MySQL or any other adapter you need. Adapters take some specific configuration, such as timeout options and pool settings, so we recommend you review the documentation for the adapter you're using.

To set up the repository configuration, open config/config.exs and add the following lines. Make sure that the hostname, username, and password values will work for the database you're using.

```
config :my_app, MyApp.Repo,
  database: "my_database",
  username: "postgres",
  password: "postgres",
  hostname: "localhost"
```

The first argument of the call to config/3 should match the OTP application name we set when defining the repository. The second argument is the name of the repository module. The options :database, :username, :password and :hostname define how to connect to the database. They can be replaced with a single :url option that provides all of these values in a URL. The URL should follow this format: ecto://USERNAME:PASSWORD@HOSTNAME/DATABASE. Using the preceding values, the URL would look like this: ecto://postgres:postgres@localhost/my_database.

You may also want to the set pool_size. This specifies how many database connections the repo will keep open. By default, Ecto sets this value to 10, but you can increase this number if you're getting timeout errors when checking out connections—this can be an indication that you do not have enough open connections to handle your application's load.

For Ecto's mix tasks to be able to find the repository, we also need to add the following line to config/config.exs:

```
config :my_app, :ecto_repos, [MyApp.Repo]
```

This will ensure that all the ecto.* mix tasks will work with our project.

Adding Ecto to the Supervision Tree

We're almost there. We've added the dependencies, defined our repository, and configured it. The last step is to ensure the repository is started when the application starts. To do this, we need to add the repository to the application supervision tree.

If your project was generated with mix new --sup you should have a file lib/my_app/application.ex with the following function:

```
def start(_type, _args) do
  # List all child processes to be supervised
  children = [
    # Starts a worker by calling: MyApp.Worker.start_link(arg)
    # {MyApp.Worker, arg},
  ]

  # See https://hexdocs.pm/elixir/Supervisor.html
  # for other strategies and supported options
  opts = [strategy: :one_for_one, name: MyApp.Supervisor]
  Supervisor.start_link(children, opts)
end
```

If you didn't create your project with the --sup option, your start function will look quite different, and you'll need to add some of this boilerplate code yourself.

To ensure the repository is started with the application, we just need to add it to the list of our project's children:

```
# List all child processes to be supervised
children = [
  MyApp.Repo
]
```

Elixir 1.5 introduced child specifications, which simplified declaring the list of child processes. If you're using an older version of Elixir, you'll need to write this slightly differently:

```
# for Elixir 1.4
import Supervisor.Spec, warn: false

children = [
  supervisor(MyApp.Repo, [])
]
```

For more information on this change, see the Elixir 1.5 release notes.[2]

---

2.   https://elixir-lang.org/blog/2017/07/25/elixir-v1-5-0-released/

Using Multiple Ecto Repos

Most of the time, your apps will only have to work with one database, so you'll just need one repo. But sometimes you'll need to connect to multiple databases, and in those cases, you'll need to set up a separate repo for each database. Ecto has good support for this scenario. First, you need to create the new repo:

```
defmodule MyApp.OtherRepo do
  use Ecto.Repo, otp_app: :my_app, adapter: Ecto.Adapter.Postgres
end
```

Then you need to configure it, just like you did with the first repo:

```
config :my_app, MyApp.OtherRepo, ...
```

```
config :my_app, :ecto_repos, [MyApp.Repo, MyApp.OtherRepo]
```

Finally, add the new repo to your application's supervision tree:

```
children = [
  MyApp.Repo,
  MyApp.OtherRepo
]
```

You can repeat this process as many times as needed for all the databases your app needs to communicate with.

That wraps up all of the configuration—let's take our app for a spin.

Starting Your App

To test our app, we need to fetch dependencies and compile the application:

```
> mix do deps.get, compile
Running dependency resolution...
...
```

If your database already exists, you can start working with Ecto right away. Test it out by running a simple query, like getting the row count of one of your tables:

```
MyApp.Repo.aggregate("some_table", :count, :some_column)
```

If don't have a database yet, you can create it using the ecto.create mix task:

```
> mix ecto.create
The database for MyApp.Repo has been created
```

If that succeeds, then your configuration is working and Ecto is able to communicate with your database.

Wrapping Up

Congratulations! You now have a brand new Elixir app that's ready to work directly with a relational database. A good next step would be to start creating migrations to fill out your database structure. If you need a refresher, see Chapter 6, Making Changes to Your Database, on page 101 for more details.

## CHAPTER 8

Working with Changesets and Phoenix Forms

If you've ever worked on a Phoenix project, you may have noticed that Ecto integrates seamlessly, almost giving the impression that the two libraries were written together. However, despite outward appearances, the two libraries are decoupled and neither was built with the other specifically in mind. The clean integration is the result of a series of protocols defined in Phoenix, and the phoenix_ecto package, which provides implementations of those protocols for Ecto.

This package provides a number of conveniences, but in this recipe, we'll focus specifically on how it allows you to use Ecto changesets with Phoenix forms. We're going to assume that you have some basic knowledge of Phoenix and EEx (Embedded Elixir), but if you don't, the code will likely be straightforward enough for you to follow along. If you feel like you need a refresher, check out the docs for Phoenix.HTML.Form.[1]

Generating a Form for a Single Schema

Let's set up a simple User schema to use as a starting point. We'll define fields for name and age and add a changeset function that will cast and validate incoming parameters:

---

1. https://hexdocs.pm/phoenix_html/Phoenix.HTML.Form.html

```
priv/examples/phoenix_forms_01.exs
defmodule MyApp.User do
  import Ecto.Changeset
  use Ecto.Schema

  schema "users" do
    field :name, :string
    field :age, :integer
  end

  def changeset(user, params) do
    user
    |> cast(params, [:name, :age])
    |> validate_required(:name)
    |> validate_number(:age, greater_than: 0,
        message: "you are not yet born")
  end

end
```

Next, we'll need a controller. When we invoke the new action on the controller, we want to return a new, empty changeset for a User:

```
def new(conn, _params) do
  changeset = User.changeset(%User{}, %{})
  render(conn, changeset: changeset)
end
```

Now we're ready to set up the form. To build forms from changesets, we use the form_for/4 function from Phoenix.HTML.Form:

```
<%= form_for @changeset, user_path(@conn, :create), fn f -> %>
  Name: <%= text_input f, :name %>
  Age: <%= number_input f, :age %>
  <%= submit "Submit" %>
<% end %>
```

Notice how we can pass our changeset directly into form_for as the first argument. If you looked at the documentation, you'd see that form_for expects Phoenix.HTML.FormData as its first argument. This is the power of Elixir protocols at work. Phoenix defined a *behavior* that it expects in Phoenix.HTML.FormData, and the phoenix_html package provides an implementation of that behavior that makes changesets act like FormData.

The second argument of form_for/4 is the action URL. This is where the request will be sent when the form is submitted. user_path(@conn, :create) points to the :create action in the UserController so let's implement that now:

```
def create(conn, %{"user" => user_params}) do
  case Accounts.create_user(user_params) do
    {:ok, user} ->
      conn
      |> put_flash(:info, "User created successfully.")
      |> redirect(to: user_path(conn, :show, user))
    {:error, %Ecto.Changeset{} = changeset} ->
      render(conn, "new.html", changeset: changeset)
  end
end
```

First, we get the parameters for the user form with params["user"]. By default, Phoenix creates HTML input names that are indexed by the schema name. For example, the age field has the input name user[age], which we access as params["user"]["age"] in Elixir. This namespacing keeps the params that are part of our %User{} changeset separate from any other params that might appear in the form.

Next, we want to take the "user" params and create a new User record. For this example, we'll assume that we've created an Accounts context that provides functions for managing User records. We pass the params to the create_user function and check the return value. If the operation succeeds, we redirect users to their profile page. If it fails, we send users back to the form, along with the failing changeset returned by create_user. This changeset has all of the values submitted by the user, so the form fields will be pre-populated with those values automatically.

Let's drop down a level and see how we might implement the create_user function:

```
def create_user(attrs \\ %{}) do
  %User{}
  |> User.changeset(attrs)
  |> Repo.insert()
end
```

We create a new changeset with the params from our controller and pass it into Repo.insert. Our controller function is already set up to receive the possible return values from insert: {:ok, user} or {:error, changeset}.

Displaying Changeset Errors

Our form is working well, but something is missing. If the user submits invalid data, the call to Repo.insert will fail, but we currently have no way of showing the user how to fix the problem. The changeset contains the validation errors, so we just need to add some elements to the page to display them. Let's do that now.

We'll start by adding a new helper function error_tag/2. This function is not provided by default so we need to define it ourselves. You can add it to any module you're using for storing helper functions.

```
priv/examples/phoenix_forms_02.exs
def error_tag(form, field) do
  if error = form.errors[field] do
    content_tag(:span, translate_error(error))
  end
end

defp translate_error({msg, opts}) do
  Enum.reduce(opts, msg, fn {key, value}, msg ->
    String.replace(msg, "%{#{key}}", to_string(value))
  end)
end
```

The function renders a <span> tag with an error message, but only if the given field actually has an error; if it doesn't, the function returns nothing.

We also defined a translate_error/1 function. We need this because Ecto stores validation errors in the format {String.t, [Keyword.t]}; for example, {"must be greater than %{number}", [number: 0]}. This may seem unnecessarily complex, but it makes it easier to translate error messages into other languages. But rather than do a deep dive into internationalization, we'll just display an English string for now.

With our helper functions in hand, we are now ready to add the error tags to the form:

```
<%= form_for @changeset, user_path(@conn, :create), fn f -> %>
  Name: <%= text_input f, :name %> <%= error_tag f, :name %>
  Age: <%= number_input f, :age %> <%= error_tag f, :age %>
  <%= submit "Submit" %>
<% end %>
```

If any of the fields contain validation errors, the user will see an error message next to the problematic input. Otherwise, error_tag will be blank.

Creating a Form with an Association

Now let's tackle a more complex case: creating a form with associations. To make it even more interesting, we'll use an embedded schema representing the user's address. If you need to refresh your memory on schemas, associations or embeds, you might want to flip back to Chapter 3, Connecting Your Tables to Elixir Structs with Schemas, on page 41 before proceeding.

First, create an embedded schema for the user's address, along with a changeset function:

```
priv/examples/phoenix_forms_03.exs
defmodule MyApp.Address do
  import Ecto.Changeset
  use Ecto.Schema

  embedded_schema do
    field :street, :string
    field :city, :string
  end

  def changeset(address, params) do
    cast(address, params, [:street, :city])
  end
end
```

Next, add the association to your %User{} schema. For now, we're only going to allow the user to have one address, so we'll use embeds_one:

```
schema "users" do
  field :name, :string
  field :age, :integer

  embeds_one :address, Address
end
```

We'll also need to modify our User.changeset function to handle the address:

```
def changeset(user, params) do
  user
  |> cast(params, [:name, :age])
  |> cast_embed(:address)
  |> validate_number(:age, greater_than: 0,
      message: "you are not yet born")
end
```

As we saw earlier, the cast function takes the user params and generates a changeset for a %User{}. cast_embed is similar—it starts with the user changeset, finds the params that belong to the :address schema, then creates a changeset for %Address{} within the %User{} changeset.

Now we need to add the address inputs to our form. We'll use the inputs_for/4 function to create a sub-form for the embedded address association:

```
<%= form_for @changeset, user_path(@conn, :create), fn f -> %>
  Name: <%= text_input f, :name %> <%= error_tag f, :name %>
  Age: <%= number_input f, :age %> <%= error_tag f, :age %>
  <%= inputs_for f, :address, fn fa -> %>
    Street: <%= text_input fa, :street %> <%= error_tag fa, :street %>
    City: <%= text_input fa, :city %> <%= error_tag fa, :city %>
  <% end %>
  <%= submit "Submit" %>
<% end %>
```

inputs_for works a lot like form_for—it acts as a kind of wrapper around the individual form inputs. But instead of passing in a changeset, we pass in the parent form, plus the name of the association and an anonymous function that contains the text_input function calls. There's no visual indication to the user that this sub-form is any different from the rest of the form, but code makes it clear that we're working with an associated schema.

Creating a Form with Multiple Associations

Let's take this one step further. In the last example, we were working with a single address via the embeds_one association. Let's try adding support for multiple addresses (embeds_many).

The process is similar to having just a single address. The inputs_for function is smart enough to handle associations with one record or with many records; it will always generate as many sub-forms as needed. So if, for example, we had two addresses associated with the user record, inputs_for would create two sub-forms, one for each address.

There's just one problem: we don't have a way for users to add a new address.

Think about how things work with just one address. When users first fill out the form, the address fields are blank. When users complete the form successfully and come back to it later, the form fields contain the data they entered before, and they can make edits if they wish. But with multiple addresses, we have to consider two possibilities: editing an existing address and creating a new one.

If we want to allow the user to add a new address, we have a few options. We could send the user to a separate page with an empty address form, or we could use JavaScript to add a form dynamically. But Phoenix has an even simpler option for us: we can use the :prepend or :append options to add an empty %Address{} to the list of associated addresses. Assuming we chose :append, the code would look like this:

```
priv/examples/phoenix_forms_03.exs
<%= inputs_for f, :address, append: [%Address{}], fn fa -> %>
  Street: <%= text_input fa, :street %> <%= error_tag fa, :street %>
  City: <%= text_input fa, :city %> <%= error_tag fa, :city %>
<% end %>
```

If we had two addresses already saved with our user record, this code would display sub-forms for those two addresses; then, since we're using the append: option, it would add a sub-form for a new, empty address after the two other addresses (if we used prepend: the new form would appear at the top). This ensures that users will always have a blank form they can use to add a new address.

Bear in mind that these options only take effect when the changeset has no parameters—when rendering a form with validation errors, Phoenix will not add the extra empty sub-form.

Wrapping Up

This covers the basics of working with Ecto and Phoenix forms. Forms are a much bigger topic that we can really cover here, so if you'd like learn more, we recommend checking out the documentation for the Phoenix.HTML.Form package.[2]

For more information on working with embedded associations in Phoenix forms, José Valim has an excellent blog post on the subject: "Working with Ecto associations and embeds."[3]

Finally, if you'd like to take deeper dive into Phoenix itself, we recommend *Programming Phoenix ≥ 1.4 [TV18]* by Chris McCord, José Valim, and Bruce Tate.

---

2. https://hexdocs.pm/phoenix_html/Phoenix.HTML.Form.html
3. http://blog.plataformatec.com.br/2015/08/working-with-ecto-associations-and-embeds/

## CHAPTER 9

Testing with Sandboxes

This chapter will show you how to turbo-charge your test suite with *sandboxes*.

Sandboxes allow you to run your database tests concurrently, while still keeping the database state of each test isolated from the others. The secret sauce underlying this feature is a special pool of database connections with an ownership mechanism that allows you to control how connections are used and shared between processes. Using the sandbox can significantly reduce the time it takes to run your test suite, so you should take advantage of this feature when you can.

We'll walk through the basics of setting up sandboxes, and show you what to do if your tests need connections shared across multiple processes. By the end, your machine will be zipping through your test suite at top speed—you'll need to find another excuse to go get coffee.

Setting Up an Async Test

To use the sandbox, change your Repo configuration to use the sandbox pool. We only want to do this when we're in our test environment, so make the following change in config/test.exs and only there:

```
priv/examples/sandboxes_01.exs
config :music_db, MusicDB.Repo,
  pool: Ecto.Adapters.SQL.Sandbox
  # other settings here
```

By changing the pool: setting, we're telling Ecto that we will not be using the default connection pool and instead give the sandbox full control over how connections are checked out and used by processes.

Next, we need to set our sandbox to the correct ownership mode. We'll cover this setting in more detail later, but for now, add this line to test/test_helper.exs:

```
Ecto.Adapters.SQL.Sandbox.mode(MusicDB.Repo, :manual)
```

Now we're ready to write our test case. Create a file called test/album_test.exs, and add the following code:

```
defmodule MusicDB.AlbumTest do
  use ExUnit.Case, async: true

  setup do
    :ok = Ecto.Adapters.SQL.Sandbox.checkout(MusicDB.Repo)
  end

  test "insert album" do
    album = MusicDB.Repo.insert!(%MusicDB.Album{title: "Giant Steps"})
    new_album = MusicDB.Repo.get!(MusicDB.Album, album.id)
    assert new_album.title == "Giant Steps"
  end
end
```

Notice that we set async: true on the first line of the test. This tells Elixir that it's safe to run this test concurrently with other tests.

We also added a setup block that calls the checkout function on the sandbox. This is how we obtain the database connection that we'll be using throughout our test. We need to make this call because we set the ownership mode to :manual in our test helper, but that's not the case for all of the ownership modes. Let's take a look at the different ownership modes we can use.

Changing the Ownership Mode

The ownership mode affects the way the sandbox interacts with different processes. You can use three different modes: :auto, :manual, and :shared.

With :auto the sandbox functions like a normal pool: each process gets its own connection from the pool and has exclusive access to the connection while it is checked out. And, like a normal pool, the connections are checked out automatically when your code needs to run a database operation, and checked back in when the operation completes. The connection is still in a sandboxed transaction that is rolled back when the connection is checked in, but you can't be sure that you'll get the same connection each time you access the database. This means that there's no guarantee that our calls to insert! and get! in our test case will use the same connection; if they use different connections, the get! call will fail when it can't find the album we inserted in the other connection.

Use :auto when you don't need to retain the state of your database throughout your test case. For example, if you're only making one database call in the test, or the result of a database call isn't dependent on the result of previous database calls, :auto is a good choice. This will likely be rare, however.

In :manual mode, which we used in the previous example, the connection is explicitly checked out in the setup block; and is not checked back in until the test exits. In this mode we can be sure that we're only using a single connection through our whole test. Any changes we make in one part of the test will be available to all the other parts, and everything will get rolled back at the end of the test.

Use :manual when you're making multiple database calls in your test case, and later calls are dependent on the result of earlier calls. It's also important that the database calls are run from the same Elixir process.

For tests that use multiple processes, Ecto has :shared mode. So far, our examples have only used one process, but consider an example like this:

```
priv/examples/sandboxes_02.exs
test "insert album" do
  task = Task.async(fn ->
    album = MusicDB.Repo.insert!(%MusicDB.Album{title: "Giant Steps"})
    album.id
  end)

  album_id = Task.await(task)
  assert MusicDB.Repo.get(MusicDB.Album, album_id).title == "Giant Steps"
end
```

In this somewhat contrived example, we're running a database operation in a separate process using Task.async. If we tried to run this test in manual or auto mode, it would crash with the error:

```
** (DBConnection.OwnershipError) cannot find ownership process
   for #PID<0.165.0>.
```

This is because the process that's trying to connect to the database (which we initiated with Task.async) was not the process that checked out the connection. With manual or auto, only the process that checked out the connection can use it.

We can work around this limitation with :shared mode. In this mode, the connection is checked out explicitly like in manual mode but the connection is available to all processes. So if you have a test that uses multiple processes, shared mode allows a single checked-out connection to be used by all of them, and you can be sure the database state is consistent throughout the test.

When working with shared mode, the setup in test/album_test.exs is a little different:

```
setup do
  :ok = Ecto.Adapters.SQL.Sandbox.checkout(MusicDB.Repo)
  Ecto.Adapters.SQL.Sandbox.mode(MusicDB.Repo, {:shared, self()})
end
```

In addition to setting the mode as :shared, we need to provide the process that's checking out the connection, so we pass in self() along with :shared as a tuple.

This seems like a good solution, but it comes at a cost: tests that use shared mode cannot be safely run concurrently. The connection is shared among *all* processes, so any test running concurrently could pollute the database state and cause other tests to fail. As a result, if you're using shared mode, you need to disable concurrency by removing async: true from use ExUnit.Case, async: true.

This is a reasonable trade-off if you don't have a large test suite. It's relatively easy to set up shared mode and not running a few tests concurrently won't be a huge time hit. But if you have a large test suite and need to run much of it in shared mode, this could be a significant setback. Fortunately, Ecto provides us with a way out. In the next section, we'll see how to get the best of both worlds: connections shared between multiple processes, and fast, concurrent tests.

Safely Sharing Connections with Allowances

To work around the limitations of shared mode, Ecto provides a mechanism called *allowances*. This allows us to pick and choose which processes we share our database connection with. We can keep a single database connection for all processes needed for our test, and be sure that the database state is isolated from any other tests running concurrently.

Let's go back to the test we looked at in the last section:

priv/examples/sandboxes_03.exs
```
test "insert album" do
  task = Task.async(fn ->
    album = MusicDB.Repo.insert!(%MusicDB.Album{title: "Giant Steps"})
    album.id
  end)

  album_id = Task.await(task)
  assert MusicDB.Repo.get(MusicDB.Album, album_id).title == "Giant Steps"
end
```

As we mentioned earlier, running this test in manual or auto mode will cause a crash, because the process in Task.async does not have access to the connection checked out by the test process. We need to "allow" the task to use the test process as the ownership process. We can do that with Ecto.Adapters.SQL.Sandbox.allow/4:

```
test "insert album" do
  parent = self()
  task = Task.async(fn ->
    Ecto.Adapters.SQL.Sandbox.allow(MusicDB.Repo, parent, self())
    album = MusicDB.Repo.insert!(%MusicDB.Album{title: "Giant Steps"})
    album.id
  end)

  album_id = Task.await(task)
  assert MusicDB.Repo.get(MusicDB.Album, album_id).title == "Giant Steps"
end
```

The call to allow ensures that the test and task processes share the same connection.

It would also be possible to call allow/4 from the test process, rather than the async process, but this would introduce a race condition: it's possible that the async process would call MusicDB.Repo.insert! before allow has finished executing. To prevent this, we would have to synchronize the start of the async process and the call to allow. The synchronization could look something like this:

```
test "insert album" do
  task = Task.async(fn ->
    receive do
      :continue -> :ok
    end
    album = MusicDB.Repo.insert!(%MusicDB.Album{title: "Giant Steps"})
    album.id
  end)

  Ecto.Adapters.SQL.Sandbox.allow(MusicDB.Repo, self(), task.pid)
  send(task.pid, :continue)

  album_id = Task.await(task)
  assert MusicDB.Repo.get(MusicDB.Album, album_id).title == "Giant Steps"
end
```

That works, but it does introduce some complexity into the code, so you might find it easier to call allow from within the collaborating process, as we did in the first example.

As powerful as allowances are, it may not always be possible to use them: your code may be structured such that it would be complicated to add them, or you may be using third-party libraries that aren't aware of the Ecto sandbox. In those cases you can fall back to :shared mode, but remember to run those tests synchronously by removing the :async option on use ExUnit.Case.

Wrapping Up

Sandboxes are a powerful feature that can help keep your test suite running at high speed. We covered the basics here, but it's possible that you'll run into some concurrency hiccups, depending on the complexity of your app. If you do run into issues, check out Ecto's documentation for more details on how to troubleshoot.[1]

---

1. https://hexdocs.pm/ecto_sql/Ecto.Adapters.SQL.Sandbox.html

## CHAPTER 10

Creating and Using Custom Types

In Chapter 3, Connecting Your Tables to Elixir Structs with Schemas, on page 41, we learned about the data types Ecto provides for creating schemas. Ecto uses these data types to translate values expressed in Elixir code into values that a database can store. A String value in Elixir, for example, becomes a VARCHAR when stored in a MySQL table.

Most of the time, Ecto's built-in data types will give you everything you need. But there may be times when you want to use a data type that's not directly supported by Ecto. For these cases, Ecto provides a mechanism for defining your own custom types. By implementing just a few functions, you can add support for storing any data type in your database.

In this chapter, we'll look at two different approaches for implementing custom types. For the first approach, we'll leverage one of the built-in types that Ecto provides to create new types. For the second, we'll go a little deeper and add support for a data type that Ecto knows nothing about.

Building on Top of Ecto's Types

When we talked about schemas, we had a table that showed how Ecto's types map to an Elixir type. If you use :string, for example, when defining a field, Ecto treats the value as a String on the Elixir side, then uses whatever column definition your database uses to store string values.

But if you think about it, a number of different kinds of data can be stored as a string: a date, a UUID, a list of values, even a complex collection of data in JSON. All of these can be stored as a string, but then parsed into a more meaningful type when brought into Elixir. Our first look at creating custom types handles this exact case: taking a value stored as a simple type in the database, and turning it into a different type when it's brought into Elixir.

Let's say we'd like to add support for working with dates and times in the Unix time format. We know that Ecto's datetime type can store and retrieve timestamps to and from the database, but, as of this writing, this type cannot handle the Unix format. You can cast strings in ISO-8601 format (2017-11-05T20:49:41Z), but if you tried to give it something like Date(1509914981) it wouldn't work.

To make this work, we can create a custom type built on Ecto's datetime type and create a slightly smarter version. To add our custom type, we need to create a module that implements the Ecto.Type behavior, which looks like this:

```
defmodule Ecto.Type do
  @callback type() :: Ecto.Type.t()
  @callback cast(term) :: {:ok, term} | {:error, keyword()} | :error
  @callback load(term) :: {:ok, term} | :error
  @callback dump(term) :: {:ok, term} | :error
  @callback equal?(term, term) :: boolean
end
```

We'll need to implement each of the first four functions to make our custom date type work correctly (equal is optional). Let's look at each one in detail.

First, let's sketch out our new module, and add the type function:

```
defmodule MusicDB.DateTimeUnix do
  @behaviour Ecto.Type

  def type(), do: :datetime
end
```

The type function needs to return the data type we want to use to store our custom value at the database level. This must be a type Ecto already supports. In this case, we're working with a timestamp, so we can use the :datetime type.

Next, we'll look at dump and load. These two functions are responsible for converting values to and from the database and application layer. Specifically, dump takes our Elixir value and converts it into a value that the database recognizes, and load converts the raw value pulled from the database into our Elixir value. Our DateTimeUnix type is just a friendly layer on top of Ecto's existing datetime type, so we can use some built-in Ecto functions to do this work for us:

```
defmodule MusicDB.DateTimeUnix do
  @behaviour Ecto.Type

  def type(), do: :datetime

  def dump(term), do: Ecto.Type.dump(:datetime, term)

  def load(term), do: Ecto.Type.load(:datetime, term)
end
```

If you look at the function signatures for dump and load, you can see that they receive and return term(). This is a generic term used to indicate any valid Elixir value.

Finally, we need to implement the cast function. Casting is when we take a value from an external source (for example, user input) and convert it into a format that Ecto can work with. You might remember the Ecto.Changeset.cast function from Chapter 4, Making Changes with Changesets, on page 63—we used this whenever we needed to create a new Changeset from a batch of raw external data. This is where all that hard work is done: behind the scenes, Ecto.Changeset.cast calls the cast function defined on each of Ecto's data types to perform the necessary type conversion. For our DateTimeUnix type, we'll need to implement cast so that it takes a string like Date(1509914981) and converts it into a DateTime struct:

```
defmodule MusicDB.DateTimeUnix do
  @behaviour Ecto.Type

  def type(), do: :datetime

  def dump(term), do: Ecto.Type.dump(:datetime, term)

  def load(term), do: Ecto.Type.load(:datetime, term)

  def cast("Date(" <> rest) do
    with {unix, ")"} <- Integer.parse(rest),
         {:ok, datetime} <- DateTime.from_unix(unix)
    do
      {:ok, datetime}
    else
      _ -> :error
    end
  end
  def cast(%DateTime{} = datetime), do: {:ok, datetime}
  def cast(_other), do: :error
end
```

We use pattern matching to look for a string that begins with "Date(" and then try to extract out the integer value and parse it into a DateTime. If the string doesn't match that format, or we can't pull out a valid integer, the function returns :error.

Our implementation is now complete. We can start using it by adding it to our schema definitions:

```
defmodule MusicDB.Album do
  use Ecto.Schema

  schema "albums" do
    field :last_viewed, MusicDB.DateTimeUnix
    #...
  end
end
```

In schemas we defined earlier, the second argument to field was always an atom representing the Ecto type we wanted to use. When working with a custom type, you instead provide the full name of the module that implements your type.

Let's look at another example. Say that we're storing data related to releases of software, and we'd like to track version numbers. Elixir has a built-in Version module that works with strings that follow semantic versioning conventions. You can give it a string like "2.1.2" and it can return things like the major version, minor version, patch level, and so on.

If we implement a custom type, we can store our versions as strings in the database, but have them appear as Version structs in our Elixir code.

We'll follow the same process we used before: we'll create a new module, then start filling in the required functions one by one.

```
defmodule EctoVersion do
  @behaviour Ecto.Type
end
```

The first step is to implement the type function, so we need to decide how we want the version value to be stored (and remember that we need to use one of Ecto's built-in types). Versions can always be expressed as strings, so :string seems to be sensible way to go:

```
defmodule EctoVersion do
  @behaviour Ecto.Type

  def type(), do: :string
end
```

Now we need to implement dump and load to make the conversion to and from the Version struct. For dump we can use Elixir's built-in to_string function to turn the struct into a string. For load we can use a function provided by the Version module itself to parse strings:

```elixir
defmodule EctoVersion do
  @behaviour Ecto.Type

  def type(), do: :string

  def dump(%Version{} = version), do: {:ok, to_string(version)}

  def load(string), do: Version.parse(string)
end
```

And finally, we need to implement cast. We will only support casting versions in string form, so we can use the same parse function we used in load, and return an error if we're given anything else:

```elixir
defmodule EctoVersion do
  @behaviour Ecto.Type

  def type(), do: :string

  def dump(%Version{} = version), do: {:ok, to_string(version)}
  def dump(_), do: :error

  def load(string) when is_binary(string), do: Version.parse(string)
  def load(_), do: :error

  def cast(string) when is_binary(string), do: Version.parse(string)
  def cast(_other), do: :error
end
```

And with that, our new EctoVersion type is ready to use.

As you can see, this took very little code, but it helps make our application code richer and more expressive than if we were just relying on the data types provided by the database.

If you're using a field like a string or a map that you'd like to have more semantic meaning, consider implementing a few functions to have your own custom type. It takes a small amount of work, but it can have a big impact on the readability and usability of your code.

Adding Custom Types Without the Built-In Types

So far, the custom types we've created have been built on the types already included in Ecto. By adding a layer on top of a built-in type, we can have richer data types in our Elixir code than we'd have just using the standard database types.

However, if you want to work with a data type that is not currently supported in Ecto, you'll need to go a little deeper and write your own driver extension.

To better understand how that might work, let's take a closer look at how data moves from your Elixir code to the database and back, as shown in this figure:

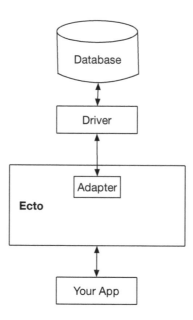

We start at the database, where the raw data is stored. Next, we have the driver, which handles converting values from the database into Elixir. Drivers are database-specific: there's an Elixir driver for Postgres, another for MySQL, and so on.

Then we get into Ecto itself. Ecto sits on top of the database drivers and implements adapters for each of the database drivers. The adapters create a uniform interface across the different databases. The API for postgrex (the Postgres driver) is very different than the API for mariaex (the driver for MySQL and MariaDB). Ecto's adapters smooth over these differences, allowing your application to use the same API, regardless of the database it's using.

If we want to use a database type that's not supported by Ecto, we'll need to drop down into the driver layer and add our customization there.

Extending database drivers is outside the scope of this book, as it would require us to cover all the different drivers that Ecto can work with. But just to give you a taste of what's involved, we'll create a small extension for Postgres that handles time intervals. (Postgrex already supports this, but we'll implement it anyway, as it's relatively small in scope and demonstrates the basics of creating an extension.)

When we implemented a custom type in the previous section, we created a module that implemented a specific behavior (Ecto.Type). The process is similar here. This time we need to implement the Postgrex.Extension behavior, and provide implementations for five different functions. Our time interval extension looks like this:

```
priv/examples/custom_types_02.exs
defmodule IntervalExtension do
  @behaviour Postgrex.Extension

  def init(_opts), do: nil

  def matching(_state), do: [send: "interval_send"]

  def format(_state), do: :binary

  def encode(_state) do
    quote do
      {months, days, seconds} ->
        microseconds = seconds * 1_000_000
        <<16::32, microseconds::64, days::32, months::32>>
    end
  end

  def decode(_state) do
    quote do
      <<16::32, microseconds::64, days :: int32, months :: int32>> ->
        seconds = div(microseconds, 1_000_000)
        {months, days, seconds}
    end
  end
end
```

The init function takes any options supplied by the user, and returns a state value that will be passed to the other behavior functions when they're called. This value can be of any type—it's only used within the extension module, so the exact details are up to the implementer of the extension. Our IntervalExtension doesn't need any state data, so we can just return nil.

The matching function tells postgrex what type we want to use the extension for. We can match directly on the type name by returning [type: "interval"] or we can match on the function PostgreSQL uses for encoding a value for the wire protocol with [send: "interval_send"]. It's usually more convenient to match on the function name, as PostgreSQL can have a generic encoder function for many different types. As long as our extension is equivalent to PostgreSQL's function we can support multiple similar types with the same extension.

The format function specifies if we want to use binary or text format for our extension. The binary format is usually more efficient and it can be used inside super types, such as arrays and records. On the other hand, the text format can be more flexible in the values it accepts, and is better documented by PostgreSQL. Trade-offs exist with either approach, so you may have to experiment to see which works better for you.

Finally we have the encode and decode functions. Unless you're familiar with Elixir meta-programming, our implementation may look a little odd. We've wrapped the logic inside a quote block, which puts the code within the block into a data structure, instead of executing the code immediately. This data structure is called an Abstract Syntax Tree or AST for short. In effect, these two functions do not actually encode and decode data directly, but rather return an AST that can do the encoding or decoding when called.

The reason for this is so that the encoder and decoder logic for all of the extensions in use can be injected into a single code block instead of being spread out over multiple modules. When the code is in a single block it is easier for the compiler to optimize it, since it can see all the code at once. Fortunately you don't have to know about meta-programming or compiler optimization to implement an extension—you just need to return the logic as an AST with the help of quote.

We'll use the tuple {months, days, seconds} to represent PostgreSQL time intervals in Elixir. For the encode/1 function we match on that exact tuple and then create a binary in the same format that PostgreSQL does for its interval_send function. The formats are not always well-documented, so you might need to find the appropriate function in the PostgreSQL source code and see how it's implemented. For the decode/1 we do the reverse: we match on the binary format and return our interval tuple.

To use the new extension, we need to define a new module with Postgrex.Types.define and include the extension we want to use. You should put this code in its own file, anywhere in your project:

```
Postgrex.Types.define(
  MyApp.PostgrexTypes,
  [IntervalExtension] ++ Ecto.Adapters.Postgres.extensions(),
  json: Jason
)
```

Then add the types option to your Repo configuration, referencing the module you created using define in the preceding snippet:

```
config :my_app, MyApp.Repo,
  types: MyApp.PostgrexTypes,
  #...
```

Now your IntervalExtension is set up and ready to use.

This was a very brief look at creating a driver extension, and it will only work for PostgreSQL. For MySQL or any other database, you would have to create separate implementations, which could look very different. But this will give you an idea of what's involved, so you can decide if it's worth the effort.

Wrapping Up

Custom types can add an extra layer of expressiveness to your Ecto projects. They allow you to use more complex types in your Elixir code than the simpler, more universal types exposed by Ecto's adapters. Building on an existing Ecto type gives you many of these benefits with a small amount of code, so it's worth consideration as you're planning out your projects.

To learn more, check out the documentation for the Ecto.Type module.[1] You might also want to explore the Hex repository[2] to look at some custom types that already exist.

---

1. https://hexdocs.pm/ecto/Ecto.Type.html
2. https://hex.pm/

## CHAPTER 11

Inserting and Updating with Upserts

Say that you wanted to front-load the genres table of your music database with every musical genre you could think of. You might choose to create a CSV file with all the data that you wanted to load, then write some code to parse the file and insert the data into the database.

At first blush, this seems pretty straightforward. You'd just need load each row of the CSV and call Repo.insert for each new record. But what if the script crashed halfway through and you wanted to run it again? Or maybe it succeeded, but you later realize that your CSV has missing or incorrect data.

To handle those scenarios, you'd have to rewrite your code. Instead of calling insert for every row in the CSV, you'd have to check the database first to see if the data was already there. If it wasn't, you'd do an insert like you did before, but if it was, you'd want to update it with the possibly new data from the CSV.

Thinking about it further, you realize that you'd have to wrap all that logic in a transaction to avoid possible race conditions. Suddenly, this is not quite as straightforward as it first seemed.

Fortunately, Ecto can do all of this heavy lifting for you through "upsert" operations.

The term "upsert" is a mash-up of "update or insert" and refers to a single operation that either updates an existing record with new data, or inserts a new record if it doesn't already exist. To do this, upserts rely on a column with a unique index, either the primary key or some other value guaranteed to be unique. When upserting a record, the system checks to see if a record with a matching unique value exists. If it does, it updates the current record; if not, it inserts a new one. This all happens atomically at the database level, avoiding potential race conditions.

In this chapter, we'll learn how to use Ecto to perform upserts. We'll work without schemas at first, then later add schemas, and see how they change the behavior.

Performing Upserts Without Schemas

To practice upserts, let's return to the genres table. This table is fairly small and has just two fields: name and wiki_tag. We can use the wiki_tag to create a link to the Wikipedia article so the user can learn more about the genre.

When we set up the table in our music_db database, we added a unique index on the name column. This ensures that we don't accidentally set up two genres with the same name—we wouldn't want to create two records for "jazz," for example. We can use this unique index to help us with our upserts.

First, let's use insert_all to create a new record for the "ska" genre:

```
priv/examples/upserts_01.exs
Repo.insert_all("genres", [[name: "ska", wiki_tag: "Ska_music"]])
# => {1, nil}
```

The 1 in the first part of the tuple tells us that one record was affected—that means our insert worked. Now let's see what happens if we try that same operation again:

```
Repo.insert_all("genres", [[name: "ska", wiki_tag: "Ska_music"]])
# => ** (Postgrex.Error) ERROR 23505 (unique_violation): duplicate key
# => value violates unique constraint "genres_name_index"
```

It blows up. In this case, that's good and it's what we expect: our unique index on name is preventing us from adding two different records with the name "ska." All good.

Now let's try doing an upsert. We can trigger the upsert behavior by adding the on_conflict option to insert_all. This option tells Ecto what it should do if it finds a record with a conflicting unique value. The default value for this option is :raise and we just saw that in action—Ecto raised an exception when we tried to insert another "ska" record.

Another possible value is :nothing, which tells Ecto that it should just ignore the conflict, and make no changes. Let's try that out:

```
Repo.insert_all("genres", [[name: "ska", wiki_tag: "Ska_music"]],
  on_conflict: :nothing)
# => {0, nil}
```

This time, we didn't get an exception, and the 0 at the beginning of the tuple tells us that no changes were made.

Differences between PostgreSQL and MySQL

All of the examples in this section demonstrate the behavior of PostgreSQL, but MySQL handles upserts differently, particularly with regard to return values. You can find detailed descriptions of the differences in Ecto's documentation,[1] so you might want to review that if you're using MySQL.

Now let's see about making a change. It turns out that we got our wiki tag wrong: it should be "Ska" rather than "Ska_music" so we want to edit our existing record. We can use the :replace option to update the record with any new values we provide. We set this option as a tuple, along with a list of the columns we'd like to update. In this case, we just want to update the :wiki_tag column:

```
Repo.insert_all("genres", [[name: "ska", wiki_tag: "Ska"]],
  on_conflict: {:replace, [:wiki_tag]}, returning: [:wiki_tag])
#=> ** (ArgumentError) :conflict_target option is required
#=> when :on_conflict is replace
```

And we get an error—not what we were expecting. The problem is that when we use the :replace option, Ecto wants us to be explicit and specify which column we want to check for uniqueness. We can fix this by adding the :conflict_target option:

```
Repo.insert_all("genres", [[name: "ska", wiki_tag: "Ska"]],
  on_conflict: {:replace, [:wiki_tag]}, conflict_target: :name,
  returning: [:wiki_tag])
# => {1, [%{wiki_tag: "Ska"}]}
```

That time, it worked, and we can see in our return value that our wiki_tag column was updated to the new value. Let's try running this exact code again, but with a new genre:

```
Repo.insert_all("genres", [[name: "ambient", wiki_tag: "Ambient_music"]],
  on_conflict: {:replace, [:wiki_tag]}, conflict_target: :name,
  returning: [:wiki_tag])
# => {1, [%{wiki_tag: "Ambient_music"}]}
```

We get the same behavior and a similar return value, but under the hood, we've inserted a new record rather than updated an existing one.

This is the main benefit of upserts: they allow us to write code that's indifferent to whether we are inserting or updating. We leave it up to the database to sort out.

---

1. https://hexdocs.pm/ecto/Ecto.Repo.html#c:insert_all/3

Another way to handle the update is to give on_conflict: a keyword list of update instructions, using the same format that the update_all function uses. With this approach, we could rewrite the previous example like this:

```
Repo.insert_all("genres", [[name: "ambient", wiki_tag: "Ambient_music"]],
  on_conflict: [set: [wiki_tag: "Ambient_music"]],
  conflict_target: :name, returning: [:wiki_tag])
```

on_conflict: will also accept an Ecto.Query struct. This is useful if you need some extra logic to determine how you want records updated.

Performing Upserts with Schemas

Just like insert_all, the insert function supports the on_conflict option for performing upserts. However, insert works with schema structs and the return value is different, so we'll have some extra considerations.

To illustrate this difference, let's reset our database with mix ecto.reset then try creating a new genre using the Genre struct:

```
priv/examples/upserts_02.exs
genre = %Genre{name: "funk", wiki_tag: "Funk"}
Repo.insert(genre)
#=> {:ok,
#=> %MusicDB.Genre{__meta__: #Ecto.Schema.Metadata<:loaded, "genres">,
#=>  albums: #Ecto.Association.NotLoaded<association :albums is not loaded>,
#=>  id: 3, inserted_at: ~N[2018-03-05 14:26:13], name: "funk",
#=>  updated_at: ~N[2018-03-05 14:26:13], wiki_tag: "Funk"}}
```

Ecto successfully inserted the new record and returned :ok, along with our new database record as a Genre struct. This is what we expect, but it's quite different than what insert_all gives us: a tuple containing the number of changed records and any values we specified in the returning: option.

Now let's use an upsert to change the wiki_tag. As before, we'll use the on_conflict: option to tell Ecto how to update the value. And because we are using PostgreSQL, we'll also use conflict_target: to specify which field contains the unique index:

```
Repo.insert(genre, on_conflict: [set: [wiki_tag: "Funk_music"]],
  conflict_target: :name)
#=> {:ok,
#=> %MusicDB.Genre{__meta__: #Ecto.Schema.Metadata<:loaded, "genres">,
#=>  albums: #Ecto.Association.NotLoaded<association :albums is not loaded>,
#=>  id: 3,inserted_at: ~N[2018-03-05 14:27:14], name: "funk",
#=>  updated_at: ~N[2018-03-05 14:27:14], wiki_tag: "Funk"}}
```

The result is surprising. Even though Ecto returned :ok it looks like our wiki_tag value hasn't changed. Moreover, the inserted_at and updated_at values have changed, even though they weren't included in our on_conflict: statement.

Let's refetch the record from the database, so we can see exactly what happened:

```
Repo.get(Genre, 3)
#=> %MusicDB.Genre{__meta__: #Ecto.Schema.Metadata<:loaded, "genres">,
#=>   albums: #Ecto.Association.NotLoaded<association :albums is not loaded>,
#=>   id: 3,inserted_at: ~N[2018-03-05 14:26:13], name: "funk",
#=>   updated_at: ~N[2018-03-05 14:26:13], wiki_tag: "Funk_music"}
```

This is more like what we were expecting: the wiki_tag value was in fact updated, and the inserted_at and updated_at values were unchanged. The database record was correct, but the return value of insert didn't reflect that.

The reason for this seemingly odd behavior is that when we use the keyword list form of on_conflict: Ecto does not reread the entire record after performing an upsert. If there's a mismatch between the values that we're updating and the values that we've asked Ecto to return, *the returned struct may not accurately reflect what's in the database.*

All is not lost, however. If you do want the struct to look exactly like the database record, you have some options.

The simplest approach is to use :replace_all or :replace_all_except_primary_key for on_conflict. These will cause all the values in the record to be replaced by the values in the struct you provide, so you need to be certain your struct is set up exactly the way you want (as the name suggests :replace_all_except_primary_key replaces everything but the primary key). These options only work with schemas, and, depending on your database, will most likely require conflict_target:

```
genre = %Genre{name: "funk", wiki_tag: "Funky_stuff"}
Repo.insert(genre, on_conflict: :replace_all_except_primary_key,
  conflict_target: :name)
#=> {:ok,
#=>  %MusicDB.Genre{
#=>    __meta__: #Ecto.Schema.Metadata<:loaded, "genres">,
#=>    albums: #Ecto.Association.NotLoaded<association :albums is not loaded>,
#=>    id: 3, inserted_at: ~N[2018-03-05 23:01:28], name: "funk",
#=>    updated_at: ~N[2018-03-05 23:01:28], wiki_tag: "Funky_stuff" }}
```

Here the return value shows our updated wiki_tag value without having to refetch the record.

If doing a replace_all on the values doesn't work, you have a few other options to ensure that the returned data matches what's in the database:

1. Use the returning option to specify a list of the fields you would like to have read back. You can also provide true rather than a list if you'd like all of the fields read.

2. When defining your schema with the field function, you can add read_after_writes: true for any fields you'd like read back. Note that this will affect *every* operation, not just upserts.

3. You can fetch the record from the database using a separate query, as we did in the preceding code.

If none of these options appeal, you might consider using insert_all rather than insert to perform the upsert. As is always the case with Ecto, using schemas may not be the most optimal approach for what you're trying to do. If something feels overly complex, bear in mind there might be another way to do it.

Wrapping Up

Upserts are a great option when you have a data loading process, like inserting the contents of CSV file, that you want to be safely repeatable. However, your data source must have at least one column with a unique index. Our genres table is ideal, as we have a unique index on the name column. But if your only unique column is the primary key, upserts may not be the right option—it would be unusual for the key to appear in a CSV file.

For more information on using upserts, see the docs for insert_all[2] and insert.[3]

---

2. https://hexdocs.pm/ecto/Ecto.Repo.html#c:insert_all/3
3. https://hexdocs.pm/ecto/Ecto.Repo.html#c:insert/2

## CHAPTER 12

Optimizing Your Application Design

Application design is a hotly debated topic. Spend a little time online and you'll find endless discussions on the subject, many ending in flame wars. In this chapter, we'll risk getting burned and offer some guidance based on what we've learned building Elixir apps with Ecto over the last few years.

We'll look at some the best practices that have emerged in the Elixir community, and see how they apply directly to Ecto. We'll cover separating pure code from impure, organizing your applications into contexts, and navigating the benefits and challenges of working with umbrella apps.

We'd like to stress that this is all subjective, and few, if any, universal rights and wrongs apply to all projects. But we hope this will give you food for thought, and guide you as you start to build out your own projects.

Separating the Pure from the Impure

A key functional programming principle is to write as much of your code as possible as pure functions, and move the impure code with side effects to the edges of your system. This is something that comes up often when working with Ecto, as database operations are the very definition of impure.

Fortunately for us, Ecto's implementation of the Repository Pattern supports this goal. Changesets, queries, and multis are pure data structures that *describe* impure actions against the database, but these actions don't take place until we run them through the functions provided by Repo. This creates a clear distinction between code that has side effects and code that doesn't. If we're just manipulating the data structures Ecto provides (for example, building up a changeset), we can consider that code "pure." But as soon as the Repo is involved, the code is likely to have side effects and should be considered "impure."

One benefit of this arrangement is that it helps us streamline our tests. Consider the following test case, which verifies that our Album module generates the correct changeset (we added a changeset function to the Album module back in Creating New Records with Associations, on page 81—you'll need to do that for this test to work, if you haven't already):

```
test/music_db/album_test.exs
test "valid changeset" do
  params = %{"title" => "Dark Side of the Moon"}
  changeset = Album.changeset(%Album{}, params)
  album = Repo.insert!(changeset)
  assert album.title == "Dark Side of the Moon"
end
```

This test expects that if we call the Album.changeset function with a map containing an album title, it will generate a changeset that inserts an album into the database. We verify that by inserting the record and making sure it has the title we expect.

There's nothing particularly wrong with this test, but it's doing more than it needs to. The purpose of the test is to make sure that our code generates the right changeset, but by calling Repo.insert! we're not just testing our function: we're testing Ecto's ability to convert our changeset into a database operation. Ecto has pretty good test coverage on its own, so maybe we don't need to duplicate that layer of testing, particularly when database calls are as time-consuming as they are.

We can eliminate the database call by rewriting the test to focus just on our changeset:

```
test/music_db/album_test.exs
test "valid changeset without insert" do
  params = %{"title" => "Dark Side of the Moon"}
  changeset = Album.changeset(%Album{}, params)
  album = Ecto.Changeset.apply_changes(changeset)
  assert album.title == "Dark Side of the Moon"
end
```

The only difference here is that instead of calling Repo.insert! we call Ecto.Changeset.apply_changes. This function takes the changes contained in the changeset and applies them directly to the underlying schema struct. We can then examine the returned struct to make sure that it contains the changes we expect.

This a small adjustment but it's a significant one. By eliminating the call to Repo we're keeping the test focused on our own code, and avoiding an expensive round-trip to the database. This can significantly reduce the amount of time it takes to run your test suite, particularly as your codebase starts to grow.

Another benefit of Ecto's separation of pure and impure operations is that it helps with code organization.

As a general rule, we recommend putting the pure functions that manipulate queries, changesets, and multis into their associated schema modules. For example, functions that generate changesets for Album structs would go into the module where we define the Album schema. That seems straightforward enough, but it leaves the question of where the impure code should go. Fortunately, recent developments in the Elixir and Phoenix communities have given us a path forward: context modules.

Working with Contexts

Phoenix 1.3 introduced the idea of contexts to the Elixir community. The Phoenix team was inspired by the concept of "bounded contexts" as described by Eric Evans in his book *Domain-Driven Design*. This pattern suggested a new way of structuring applications, and the team updated Phoenix's generators so that contexts became the default behavior.

With contexts, we can group related functionality. A context consists of a single main module, usually referred to as the context module, and, optionally, a directory with more modules that help implement the functionality of the context. A context may have many modules or just one, but in either case, the context module contains the external interface of the context.

This is not a new pattern, and it's not unique to Phoenix applications. In fact, the Ecto library itself uses contexts. For example, the Ecto.Query module is the external interface for building and manipulating queries. Several other internal modules are under the same namespace (Ecto.Query.Builder, Ecto.Query.Planner, and others), but you generally don't work with those modules directly. Ecto.Query contains the API that you call, and the other modules provide support to make that API work.

Organizing Your Code with Ecto and Contexts

For our own apps that use Ecto, contexts help us divide the pure code from the impure. We recommend putting all impure code (that is, code that uses Repo) into the context module, and putting the pure code (manipulations of changesets, queries, and the like) into schema modules that live in the context's namespace.

Let's look at how we might start implementing a Music context for our MusicDb app:

```
priv/examples/appdesign_01.exs
# lib/music_db/music.ex
defmodule MusicDB.Music do
  alias MusicDB.Music.{Repo, Album, Artist}

  def get_artist(name) do
    MusicDB.Repo.get_by(Artist, name: name)
  end

  def all_albums_by_artist(artist) do
    Ecto.assoc(artist, :albums)
    |> MusicDB.Repo.all()
  end

  def search_albums(string) do
    string
    |> Album.search()
    |> MusicDB.Repo.all()
  end
end
```

We've created a top-level context module called MusicDb.Music and provided a few functions we think we might need: get_artist, all_albums_by_artist, and so on. We then move the schema modules (in this case, Album and Artist) into the MusicDb.Music namespace, and add any supporting functions needed by the context module:

```
priv/examples/appdesign_01.exs
# lib/music_db/music/artist.ex
defmodule MusicDB.Music.Artist do
  use Ecto.Schema

  schema "artists" do
    field :name, :string
    has_many :albums, MusicDB.Music.Album
  end
end

# lib/music_db/music/album.ex
defmodule MusicDB.Music.Album do
  use Ecto.Schema
  import Ecto.Query
  alias MusicDB.Music.{Album, Artist}

  schema "albums" do
    field :title, :string
    belongs_to :artist, Artist
  end
```

```
  def search(string) do
    from album in Album,
      where: ilike(album.title, ^"%#{string}%")
  end
end
```

This helps us in two ways. First, it gives us a clear and consistent method for separating pure code from impure—we always know which parts of our code hit the database and which don't. Second, it allows clients of our context (that is, other parts of our code) to be agnostic about how our data is stored. We could swap out Ecto for some other data access library and the rest of our code would still work. Provided our API delivers as advertised, the rest of the codebase doesn't need to know how we're storing the data.

Best Practices for Contexts

Contexts can go a long way toward making your codebase easier to work with, but a few general guidelines can help maximize their benefit.

As much as possible, treat the context module as the external API of the context, and consider the supporting modules private. You have, of course, no way to enforce this, and it's likely that the context will return structs defined in the supporting modules (especially if your context contains Ecto schemas). But from outside of the context, we should try to call the functions on the context module exclusively, and leave the other modules alone.

Contexts are a grouping mechanism so we should not put all our modules into the same context unless our application is very small. Say we decided to extend our MusicDb application to include a forum where users could comment on albums they like (or don't). In that case, we would add new contexts to support these features. The forum logic with Post and Comment schemas could go into a Forum context, and the user account logic with User and authentication code could go into an Accounts context. Anytime you start adding new modules to your codebase, you should consider whether it might be time to add a new context.

We all know that naming things is hard, and it's the same for contexts. If you are unable to find a good name for your context, you can try taking the most prominent module in the context and pluralizing it. As an example, the main module in an Accounts context would probably be the User module, so we could also name the context Users.

Contexts are supposed to group related concerns into distinct sections of your application, but you will inevitably get dependencies between the contexts you have defined, where modules reference each other. This is a particular concern as we start adding associations between our schemas. Cross-context dependencies indicate that the contexts are coupled, which we want to avoid as much as possible. If you have a high number of dependencies across contexts, it may suggest that your contexts have the wrong boundaries.

It can sometimes be hard to know which context a module belongs to. We try to keep our contexts small, so if you are creating a new module and don't find a context where it fits, you should probably create a new context for it. You may not get it exactly right the first time, and when your application grows, the contexts may not fit as well as they used to. As with all software, it is an ongoing effort to refactor your code as the app evolves, so you will likely need to restructure your contexts to make sure they follow these principles.

Working with Umbrella Applications

Contexts can help you determine how to break your app into more manageable parts. But as your app continues to grow, you may find that you want a greater degree of separation between the components. This can happen if individual contexts start to grow too large, or if you just want to be able to deploy different parts of your app separately.

Umbrellas allow you to easily group multiple applications into the same mix project and source code repository. Instead of bundling all of our code into a single application, we can split it up into multiple applications. Elixir's mix new and Phoenix's mix phx.new generators support creating umbrella projects by passing the --umbrella flag.

Understanding Umbrellas

An umbrella project consists of a top-level mix project (usually called the umbrella project) and several sub-projects inside the apps/ directory (usually called child applications).

What's in a Name?

When working with Elixir and OTP, terminology can get a little confusing, particularly with the words "project" and "application." In this case, a "project" is something we use to configure and organize the app we're building, and "application" is an OTP application. You can find out more about these terms in the Elixir guides.[1]

---

1. https://elixir-lang.org/getting-started/mix-otp/introduction-to-mix.html

The umbrella project is what we use to configure and organize our application, through the mix.exs and config/ files. All of the logic and code that makes the app work reside in the child applications.

Usually a mix project is also an OTP application, but that's not the case for the top-level umbrella project—only projects inside the apps/ directory are actual OTP applications. This means the umbrella project should only be used for configuring the other applications, and no application code should live inside it.

One way to use umbrellas is to split the front-end and back-end logic into separate applications:

```
music_umbrella/ (Mix project)
  - mix.exs
  - ...
  - apps/
    - music/ (Mix project / OTP application)
      - mix.exs
      - ...
    - music_web/ (Mix project / OTP application)
      - mix.exs
      - ...
```

Since the front-end application music_web depends on the back-end application music, we declare it as a dependency inside apps/music_web/mix.exs:

priv/examples/appdesign_02.exs
```
def deps() do
  [{:music, in_umbrella: true}]
end
```

This also has the nice effect that if we add more front ends to our application, for example RPC over a non-web protocol, we can keep them completely separate in different applications.

Most tooling around Mix understands umbrellas, which makes them easy to use when building releases and deploying code. You can tell your release builder to include only specific applications in your umbrella, so you could deploy your different front ends separately.

Considerations When Working with Ecto

Switching from a single OTP application to an umbrella can be a life-saver as your app starts to grow and becomes harder to manage. But it does come at the cost of some added complexity, and you'll have to give some thought to the dependencies between applications.

In the last section, we talked about adding Accounts and Forums contexts to our app. Let's imagine that those contexts got large enough that we decided to split them out into their own applications.

One of the first things we'd run into is that they both need access to the Repo. When they were contexts within the same application, the MusicDb.Repo module was easy enough to share, but that won't be the case when they're in separate applications.

We can fix this by moving the MusicDb.Repo module into its own music_repo application that the other applications will access as a dependency. This change will let us keep the repository configuration in a single place, making it easier to update if we need to. It also means that we'll have a single pool of connections that the other applications will share, which will reduce our resource usage.

With this change, our umbrella will have the following applications:

```
music_umbrella/
  - apps/
    - music_repo/
    - music_accounts/
    - music_forum/
    - music/
    - music_web/
```

Let's think about the relationship between music_accounts and music_forum. The forum application will have to depend on the accounts application because you need an account to post on the forum. But accounts should not depend on a forum because you don't need the forum for account tasks such as authentication. You can't have cyclic dependencies between applications, so you can strictly enforce the unidirectional relationship between forums and accounts.

With that in mind, our dependency tree would look something like this diagram:

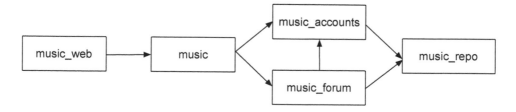

This will work, but it introduces a snag. Let's consider the following schema definitions:

```
priv/examples/appdesign_02.exs
defmodule Forum.Post do
  use Ecto.Schema

  schema "posts" do
    belongs_to :user, Accounts.User
  end
end

defmodule Accounts.User do
  use Ecto.Schema

  schema "user" do
    # This is not allowed due to the one-directional relationship
    # has_many :posts, Forum.Post
  end
end
```

It seems natural to create a has-many/belongs-to relationship between users and posts. And if we defined these two schemas within the same application, that's exactly what we'd do. But we've split them out, and in our new arrangement, the User schema can't access the Post schema.

This doesn't have to be a dealbreaker, however. Remember that creating associations in schemas merely provides us with some conveniences, but we have other ways to accomplish similar tasks. For example, one thing we can't do without the has_many association is use assoc(user, :posts) to get all of the posts for a particular user. But with a few more lines of code, we can create the same functionality by implementing it on the Post side, rather than the User side:

```
priv/examples/appdesign_02.exs
defmodule Forum.Post do
  use Ecto.Schema
  import Ecto.Query

  # ...

  def from_user(user_or_users) do
    # assoc() can take a single schema or a list - we'll do the same
    user_ids = user_or_users |> List.wrap() |> Enum.map(& &1.id)
    from p in Post,
      where: p.user_id in ^user_ids
  end
end
```

This is a workaround, and it's perhaps not intuitive if you're used to the convenience of using assoc. As of this writing, Ecto does not have much support for working with umbrellas, and the community is still working out what some best practices might be. Future versions of Ecto may address some of these challenges more directly. In the meantime, remember that Ecto is flexible and there's often more than one way to do things. You should feel free to experiment, and share what you find with the community.

Wrapping Up

Application design is a big topic, and we've really just scratched the surface here. But we hope we've given you some ideas that will help inform the choices you make as your projects evolve over time.

We recommend following the functional programming principle of separating pure code from impure; for Ecto, that means keeping code that touches Repo separate from code that doesn't. Working with contexts can help, as you can put the code that uses Repo into the context module, and put the schema definitions into separate modules in the same namespace. If you're using umbrellas, we recommend putting your Repo module into a separate child application that can be shared by its siblings.

If you'd like to learn more about contexts, the official Phoenix guide has a lot of good information.[2]

For more details about umbrellas, check out the documentation on the official Elixir site.[3]

---

2. https://hexdocs.pm/phoenix/contexts.html
3. https://elixir-lang.org/getting-started/mix-otp/dependencies-and-umbrella-projects.html

## CHAPTER 13

Working with Embedded Schemas

Embedded schemas are an alternative to using associations. Unlike regular associations, embedded schemas are stored on the same record as the parent schema, rather than a separate table. They are "embedded" in the parent schema.

Choosing embedded schemas (or "embeds") over associations has advantages in some use cases, but working with them is a little different. In this chapter, we'll go over how to create and manage embeds, and we'll discuss why you might (or might not) want to use them.

Please note that the examples in this chapter will not work with MySQL. At the database level, we'll be using the array column type to store embedded "has many" relationships, and as of this writing, MySQL does not support arrays without jumping through a few extra hoops. To keep the examples clearer, we're taking an approach that only works with Postgres.

Creating Embedded Schemas

To try out embeds, we're going to veer slightly from the data model we've been working with so far. We're going to create a new Album schema. This one will use embeds, rather than associations, to handle the child records for Artist and Track. The relationships will still be the same (that is, albums will have have one artist, and have many tracks) but we'll model these relationships using embeds.

To keep this approach distinct in our codebase, we'll create new schemas with different names. Let's start with tracks.

You define embeds similarly to normal schemas, but you don't provide a name for the source table, since they belong to no particular table:

lib/music_db/track_embed.ex
```
defmodule MusicDB.TrackEmbed do
  import Ecto.Changeset
  use Ecto.Schema

  embedded_schema do
    field(:title, :string)
    field(:duration, :integer)
  end
end
```

The other difference is that the default type for the primary key is binary_id instead of id. binary_id's are represented by an automatically generated UUID, rather than auto-incrementing integers. This is because auto-incrementing integers can only be declared on the column level, not for data inside a column.

Let's also create an embed for artist records:

lib/music_db/artist_embed.ex
```
defmodule MusicDB.ArtistEmbed do
  import Ecto.Changeset
  use Ecto.Schema

  embedded_schema do
    field(:name)
  end
end
```

In most respects, declaring an embed is not much different from a regular schema. Calling embedded_schema instead of schema is the key difference.

Adding Embeds to Another Schema

Now let's set up the album schema that will use these embeds. This will be a regular schema, similar to what we've worked with earlier. We'll need a new database table to go with it, as we're storing our child records with embeds rather than associations.

Here's what our new migration looks like:

priv/repo/migrations/20180516132926_add_albums_with_embeds.exs
```
def change do
  create table("albums_with_embeds") do
    add(:title, :string)
    add(:artist, :jsonb)
    add(:tracks, {:array, :jsonb}, default: [])
  end
end
```

The Ecto types for embeds are :map (for has-one relationships) and {:array, :map} (for has-many). At the database level, we use json (or possibly jsonb for PostgreSQL) when storing maps, so that's the type we specified in our migration.

Since we're using JSON for the backing storage, all values in an embedded schema must be able to encode and decode to and from JSON. This works out of the box for all of Ecto's built-in types, but you'll need to double-check this if you're using any custom Ecto types (we talk about custom types in Chapter 10, Creating and Using Custom Types, on page 145).

You may have noticed that we set the default for tracks to "[]". This is so that even if we have no tracks when creating the album, we will store an empty list. Ecto will translate NULL values to an empty list to keep the behavior the same as has_many, but we still recommend keeping the database and application data as close as possible, so we use a default.

Now we can set up the schema for our new table:

```
lib/music_db/album_with_embeds.ex
defmodule MusicDB.AlbumWithEmbeds do
  use Ecto.Schema
  alias MusicDB.{ArtistEmbed, TrackEmbed}

  schema "albums_with_embeds" do
    field :title, :string
    embeds_one :artist, ArtistEmbed, on_replace: :update
    embeds_many :tracks, TrackEmbed, on_replace: :delete
  end

end
```

To add embeds to another schema you use embeds_one/3 or embeds_many/3. embeds_one is the counterpart to has_one for associations, as is embeds_many to has_many. There is no equivalent function for belongs_to. Because embeds reside in the same database records as their parent, we don't use the foreign keys that are a critical component of belongs_to.

Interestingly, you can put embeds inside other embeds; if we changed schema "albums" to embedded_schema in the preceding example it would work just as well.

The seed data for the MusicDB app includes one AlbumWithEmbeds record. We can fetch that record and see what we get back:

```
priv/examples/embedded_schemas_02.exs
Repo.get_by(AlbumWithEmbeds, title: "Moanin'")
#=> %MusicDB.AlbumWithEmbeds{
#=>   __meta__: #Ecto.Schema.Metadata<:loaded, "albums_with_embeds">,
```

```
#=>   artist: %MusicDB.ArtistEmbed{
#=>     id: "cab33f94-ecfb-461e-83a8-5ace0e02b9ca",
#=>     name: "Art Blakey"
#=>   },
#=>   id: 1,
#=>   title: "Moanin'",
#=>   tracks: [
#=>     %MusicDB.TrackEmbed{
#=>       duration: 575,
#=>       id: "7a8ae464-68fc-4320-a1a1-f555b3be74ba",
#=>       title: "Moanin'"
#=>     },
#=>     %MusicDB.TrackEmbed{
#=>       duration: 290,
#=>       id: "551a4623-a1eb-4bbc-9d30-024e3fce10e2",
#=>       title: "Are You Real"
#=>     },
#=>     ...
```

We have truncated the output a bit, but also notice that we got the embedded ArtistEmbed and TrackEmbed records without having to call preload. The database stores the parent and child records in the same row, so fetching the parent record pulls them all in at once.

Making Changes

Now let's look at making some changes to our embedded records. Because the data is embedded in the parent record, it's tempting to think that you can simply manipulate the records the same as the other fields in the schema. But this is not the case. You must always use changesets when working with embeds, and work with the specialized functions that Ecto provides: put_embed/4 and cast_embed/3. In the database, the child records are stored in a column, but in our Elixir code, it's more accurate to think of embeds like associations.

put_embed/4 and cast_embed/3 work just like their counterparts put_assoc/4 and cast_assoc/3 so we need to give some thought to the :on_replace option when setting up our embeds. The values available for :on_replace are :raise (the default), :mark_as_invalid, :update, :delete. These work the same way as they do in associations, so you can flip back to Associations Using Internal Data, on page 77 if you need a refresher.

Working with put_embed

Just like put_assoc, put_embed is the best choice when working with internal data. put_embed accepts a struct for the embedded schema, a keyword list, map, or changeset. Let's look at an example of that:

```
priv/examples/embedded_schemas_03.exs
album = Repo.get_by(AlbumWithEmbeds, title: "Moanin'")
changeset = change(album)
changeset = put_embed(changeset, :artist, %{name: "Arthur Blakey"})
changeset = put_embed(changeset, :tracks,
  [%TrackEmbed{title: "Moanin'"}])
```

We said earlier that only changesets can be used to update embeds. This is still true even though we're passing maps and structs. Let's run part of the last example again, and look carefully at the return value:

```
album = Repo.get_by(AlbumWithEmbeds, title: "Moanin'")
changeset = change(album)
changeset = put_embed(changeset, :artist, %{name: "Arthur Blakey"})
#=> #Ecto.Changeset<
#=>   action: nil,
#=>   changes: %{
#=>     artist: #Ecto.Changeset<
#=>       action: :insert,
#=>       changes: %{name: "Arthur Blakey"},
#=>       errors: [],
#=>       data: #MusicDB.ArtistEmbed<>,
#=>       valid?: true
#=>     >
#=>   },
#=>   errors: [],
#=>   data: #MusicDB.AlbumWithEmbeds<>,
#=>   valid?: true
#=> >
```

If you look at the artist value under changes, you'll see that Ecto has converted our map into a changeset.

Working with cast_embed

cast_embed, similar to cast_assoc, works on the basis that the changes to the embed are stored in the params of the parent record's changeset. This is useful when you don't want to separately build a changeset and use put_embed to put it on the parent changeset. The cast_embed function accepts the same options as cast_assoc and they work the same way:

```
priv/examples/embedded_schemas_04.exs
album = Repo.get_by(AlbumWithEmbeds, title: "Moanin'")
params = %{
  "artist" => %{"name" => "Arthur Blakey"},
  "tracks" => [%{"title" => "Moanin'"}]
}
```

```
changeset = cast(album, params, [])
changeset = cast_embed(changeset, :artist)
changeset = cast_embed(changeset, :tracks)
```

As you may recall from Creating New Records with Associations, on page 81, we had to add a changeset/2 function to the schema modules we were casting into associations. The same goes for embeds. If you look in artist_embed.ex and track_embed.ex you'll see that we added rudimentary changeset functions so that this example would run. Just as with associations, Ecto looks to your code to find out how to cast params from external sources into schema structs.

Considerations When Skipping Primary Keys

By default, embedded_schema will add a primary key to your embed. This is useful when you want to update or remove individual items from an embeds_many association, as you have a reliable id to distinguish the records in the collection. Primary keys are optional, however, and you don't have to use them if you don't want to, but a few caveats exist that you should bear in mind.

When using embeds_many, :on_replace must be set to :delete if the embedded schema has no primary key and you wish to update the list of embeds. This is because Ecto uses the primary key to track which embeds in the list are being updated in place, or if they are being replaced by new records.

Similarly for embeds_one, if there is no primary key you have to decide if the record should be updated or replaced, by setting the value to :update or :delete, respectively. Again, this is because Ecto needs the primary key to track if the embed is being updated or replaced.

Because of these peculiarities, the Ecto teams recommends always using a primary key—this is Ecto's default behavior.

Choosing Between Embedded Schemas and Associations

Embedded schemas have some advantages over associations. Since the child records are stored with the parent, you don't have to use joins or Repo.preload to fetch them. This can help with performance, because you can avoid extra round-trips to the database. It also means the data is stored closely together on disk and in memory, reducing expensive disk seeks and increasing caching efficiency.

Another consideration is that with schemas, every time you make changes you also have to create an accompanying migration. Embeds use unstructured

JSON, so you only need to change your schema definition and leave the database alone. This is more flexible and can lead to more efficient iteration.

But embeds do not replace associations, and they can't do some things. Because they are stored in a single column, you can't do partial updates on a field-by-field by basis on the embedded schema. Ecto supports field-level changes within changesets, but under the hood, the whole schema needs to be sent to the database even if you are only updating a single field. Additionally, embeds don't use foreign keys, which means you lose the referential integrity that databases provide with foreign keys.

You may be wondering when you *should* use embeds—that's a good question and there isn't one definitive answer. In general, you should use embeds when you have unstructured data, or a structure that changes often enough that you don't want to use migrations. Embeds are also a good option when you have an association that is always or almost always fetched together with the parent schema, or when the association is small enough that it's not worth storing it separately.

Another use case for embedded_schema is when you're working with schemas that aren't backed by a database table. We'll be exploring that option in detail in Chapter 16, Using Schemas Without Tables, on page 193.

Wrapping Up

Ecto provides excellent support for working with embeds—the trick is knowing when and when not to use them. This is something that will become clear as you gain more experience working with Ecto and schemas in general. And thankfully, the APIs for embeds and associations are similar enough that changing your mind won't require a substantial rewrite.

For more information on working with embeds, see the docs for Ecto.Schema.[1]

---

1. https://hexdocs.pm/ecto/Ecto.Schema.html#embeds_one/3

## CHAPTER 14

Creating Polymorphic Associations

Let's say we wanted to add a new feature to our MusicDB app that would allow us to add notes to our album records. These notes could be anything like metadata about the album (producer, engineer, and so on), or maybe even our own personal comments.

Our first instinct might be to add a "notes" column to the albums table. But after some consideration, we realize that we'd like to allow each record to have multiple notes, perhaps written by different users. So instead of just adding a column, we decide to create a new notes table, and create a has_many/belongs_to relationship between albums and notes. So far, so good.

But as we think a little further, we realize that we'd like to add notes not just to albums but to artists and tracks as well. So we want to keep our notes table, but we want to be able create associations with more than one table.

This is a case for *polymorphic associations*. This is a special type of association that allows a single record type to have a "belongs to" relationship with more than one type of record. Unlike some database frameworks, Ecto doesn't have a specific mechanism for managing polymorphic associations, but using some of the tools we've already learned about, we can implement the notes feature we'd like to add.

In this chapter we'll look at traditional approaches to polymorphism, and discuss why Ecto doesn't follow them. We'll then outline three different approaches for implementing polymorphism in Ecto, exploring the advantages and disadvantages of each.

Polymorphism in Other Frameworks

Some frameworks, notably ActiveRecord and Laravel, have a built-in convention to support polymorphic relationships. Here's how we might follow that convention with our notes feature.

Say that our notes table started with just these two columns:

Field	Type
notes	text
author	string

To support polymorphism, we would add two more columns that would indicate the table name and ID of the record we want to attach the note to. When naming these columns, the convention is to use an adjective that's descriptive of the relationship, then add _type for the column that holds the table name, and _id for the ID. In our case, it might look like this:

Field	Type
notes	text
author	string
notable_type	string
notable_id	id

With this in place, we could add a note to the album "Kind Of Blue" (which has the ID 1), by adding this record to the notes table:

Field	Value
notes	"Love this album!"
author	"darin"
notable_type	"albums"
notable_id	1

The frameworks that support this convention allow you to define the "has-many" relationship as polymorphic, and they automatically combine the notable_type and notable_id values to load the correct record when needed.

As convenient as this arrangement may appear, it's not one that Ecto supports, and for good reasons.

First, this type of polymorphism breaks foreign key integrity constraints. Storing the table name and ID as separate database columns is not compatible with how databases manage foreign keys. In our case, our notable_id is not a true foreign key—it's just a value in a column. This means that we lose the database's built-in integrity checks, making it harder to keep our data correct.

Second, performance suffers. Looking up records with polymorphic associations is much less efficient than with regular associations. You may not notice it at first, but as your database grows, you may well run into performance problems that can be difficult to resolve without substantial rewriting.

The Ecto team members had been burned by these issues enough times that they elected not to build this type of polymorphism into Ecto. However, it's still possible to create polymorphic associations in Ecto; and the good news is you've already learned most of the tools to help you do it.

In the rest of this chapter, we'll look at three different approaches for implementing polymorphism, and consider the advantages and disadvantages of each. With this information in hand, you'll be able to evaluate which of these approaches might work best for your needs.

Approach #1: Multiple Foreign Keys

Before we dive into this approach, let's remind ourselves of the task at hand. We want to able to add notes to any artist, album, or track. Each of those records needs to be able to have any number of notes by any number of authors, which is why we elected to store the notes in a separate table, rather than add a notes column to each of the three tables.

One way to achieve this is to have a single notes table, then add separate foreign key columns for each of the tables we want to attach notes to. Our migration would look something like this:

priv/repo/migrations/20180620125250_add_notes_tables.exs
```
create table(:notes_with_fk_fields) do
  add :note, :text, null: false
  add :author, :string, null: false
  add :artist_id, references(:artists)
  add :album_id, references(:albums)
  add :track_id, references(:tracks)
  timestamps()
end
```

And our schema definition might look like this:

```
lib/music_db/note.ex
schema "notes_with_fk_fields" do
  field(:note, :string)
  field(:author, :string)
  timestamps()
  belongs_to(:artist, MusicDB.Artist)
  belongs_to(:album, MusicDB.Album)
  belongs_to(:track, MusicDB.Track)
end
```

Finally, we create the has_many side of the association by adding the following line to each of the Artist, Album, and Track schemas:

```
has_many :notes, MusicDB.Note
```

Once this is done, we're all set. We can create notes for any artist, album, or track record, and we can use all of the familiar functions for creating and querying associated records (we covered these in Adding Associations to Schemas, on page 49).

Here's how we could add and retrieve a note for an Artist record:

```
artist = Repo.get_by(Artist, name: "Bobby Hutcherson")
note = Ecto.build_assoc(artist, :notes,
  note: "My fave vibes player", author: "darin")
Repo.insert!(note)
artist = Repo.preload(artist, :notes)
artist.notes
# => [
#   %MusicDB.Note{
#     ...
#   }
#]
```

To add a note for an Album record, we can do the exact same thing:

```
album = Repo.get_by(Album, title: "Kind Of Blue")
note = Ecto.build_assoc(album, :notes,
  note: "Love this album!", author: "darin")
Repo.insert!(note)
album = Repo.preload(album, :notes)
album.notes
# => [
#   %MusicDB.Note{
#     ...
#   }
#]
```

Advantages: This is probably the simplest approach, and the easiest for someone reading your code to understand.

Disadvantages: First, you end up with unused foreign key columns. The notes table needs to have a foreign key field for each of the different tables it can attach to. But a single note record can only be attached to one other record, so for any given notes record, only one foreign key column will have a value. If you had a large number of tables that you were attaching notes to, this could get unwieldy.

You would also need to give some thought to data integrity. The foreign key fields in your notes table have to allow null values, as any note can be attached to any type of record. But it would be incorrect if they were all null or if two or more of the fields were non-null.

We can address this by adding a custom validation to our Note schema that checks to make sure that one and only one of the fields is populated. And if you're using a database that supports check constraints, you can add a constraint when you create the table to ensure that the database will enforce this logic as well.

Using Postgres, we could add this to our migration:

```
priv/repo/migrations/20180620125250_add_notes_tables.exs
fk_check = """
  (CASE WHEN artist_id IS NULL THEN 0 ELSE 1 END) +
  (CASE WHEN album_id IS NULL THEN 0 ELSE 1 END) +
  (CASE WHEN track_id IS NULL THEN 0 ELSE 1 END) = 1
"""
create constraint(:notes_with_fk_fields, :only_one_fk, check: fk_check)
```

This will ensure that one and only one of the foreign key fields is set to a non-null value.

Despite the disadvantages listed here, we believe that this is usually the best approach to take. The main reason you might not want to do it this way is if you had dozens or more different tables you wanted to attach to. In that case, it might make more sense to break the associations out into individual tables, and the next two approaches will show you different ways of doing that.

Approach #2: Using an Abstract Schema

This approach might not be completely intuitive at first glance, but it's worth exploring as it reveals some interesting features about schemas that we haven't looked at before, and might be the right solution for your app.

With this approach, we'll create separate notes tables for each of the other tables we're associating with. So we'll have one notes table for artists, another for albums, and so on. Here's how we might write the migration:

priv/repo/migrations/20180620125250_add_notes_tables.exs
```
create table(:notes_for_artists) do
  add :note, :text, null: false
  add :author, :string, null: false
  add :assoc_id, references(:artists)
  timestamps()
end

create table(:notes_for_albums) do
  add :note, :text, null: false
  add :author, :string, null: false
  add :assoc_id, references(:albums)
  timestamps()
end

create table(:notes_for_tracks) do
  add :note, :text, null: false
  add :author, :string, null: false
  add :assoc_id, references(:tracks)
  timestamps()
end
```

Notice we used assoc_id for the foreign key. We deliberately chose a more abstract name, and used it in each of the tables. We did this so all of the tables have the same column names. This allows us to create a single schema struct we'll share across the three different notes tables. Our schema will look like this:

lib/music_db/note.ex
```
schema "abstract table: notes" do
  field :note, :string
  field :author, :string
  field :assoc_id, :integer
  timestamps()
end
```

We broke convention here, and did not provide a real table name with this schema. Instead, we just added a string indicating that we're using an "abstract" schema. We could have written anything here—we just need to make it clear that we're not intending to specify a database table. Instead, we'll create the connection between the schema and the database table when we define each association. For example, here's what we'll add to our Artist schema definition:

```
has_many :notes, {"notes_for_artists", MusicDB.Note},
  foreign_key: :assoc_id
```

This is new behavior so let's take a closer look.

In previous examples of has_many, we've always provided a schema module as the second argument. But if you look at the documentation for has_many you'll see that Ecto is not necessarily looking for a schema, but rather our old friend Queryable (which we met back in Composing Queries, on page 32). As you may recall, Ecto provides Queryable implementations for several different types, one of which is a tuple. We're taking advantage of this implementation to make this association work.

The tuple we're passing in contains the table name, and a schema module. This tells Ecto that we want to take our new Note schema and apply it to the notes_for_artists table. It's kind of like late binding for schemas and tables!

Our Album and Track schemas will follow the same pattern:

```
# lib/music_db/album.ex
has_many :notes, {"notes_for_albums", MusicDB.Note}, foreign_key: :assoc_id
```

```
# lib/music_db/track.ex
has_many :notes, {"notes_for_tracks", MusicDB.Note}, foreign_key: :assoc_id
```

Once we've done this, we can use the association just as we did with our previous approach:

```
artist = Repo.get_by(Artist, name: "Bobby Hutcherson")
note = Ecto.build_assoc(artist, :notes,
  note: "My fave vibes player", author: "darin")
Repo.insert!(note)
artist = Repo.preload(artist, :notes)
artist.notes
# => [
#   %MusicDB.Note{
#     ...
#   }
#]
```

Advantages: Having separate tables prevents having lots of unused columns like we did in the first approach. Here all the data is kept separate, so the table design is much cleaner.

Disadvantages: The columns for Note have to be repeated in each of the association tables. If we decide to add or remove a column, we have to make sure we change all of the tables together. This could be painful if we had a large number of tables to manage.

Something else to consider with this approach is that you can't create Note records directly. This, for example, won't work:

```
Repo.insert!(%Note{})
```

We can't use a Queryable here—insert! expects a struct, so there's no way for us to do our "late binding" trick and associate our Note struct with the correct database table. We have to start with the parent record and use build_assoc (as we did in the preceding code), cast_assoc, or put_assoc to create the child record.

Approach #3: Using many_to_many

The final approach for creating polymorphic associations is to use many_to_many. With this approach, we create a single notes table, then add separate join tables for each of the different associations we want to use with notes. We would set this up the same way we did back in Many-to-Many Associations, on page 53.

First, we add a migration to create a single notes table:

priv/repo/migrations/20180620125250_add_notes_tables.exs
```
create table(:notes_with_joins) do
  add :note, :text, null: false
  add :author, :string, null: false
  timestamps()
end
```

And also add migrations to create the join tables:

priv/repo/migrations/20180815192832_add_notes_join_tables.exs
```
create table(:artists_notes) do
  add :artist_id, references(:artists)
  add :note_id, references(:notes_with_joins)
end
create index(:artists_notes, :artist_id)
create index(:artists_notes, :note_id)

create table(:albums_notes) do
  add :album_id, references(:albums)
  add :note_id, references(:notes_with_joins)
end
create index(:albums_notes, :album_id)
create index(:albums_notes, :note_id)

create table(:tracks_notes) do
  add :track_id, references(:tracks)
  add :note_id, references(:notes_with_joins)
end
create index(:tracks_notes, :track_id)
create index(:tracks_notes, :note_id)
```

Then we set up the Note schema:

```
lib/music_db/note.ex
schema "notes_with_joins" do
  field :note, :string
  field :author, :string
  many_to_many :artists, MusicDB.Artist, join_through: "artists_notes"
  many_to_many :albums, MusicDB.Album, join_through: "albums_notes"
  many_to_many :tracks, MusicDB.Track, join_through: "tracks_notes"
  timestamps()
end
```

Finally, we add the association to our Artist, Album, and Track schemas:

```
# lib/music_db/artist.ex
many_to_many :notes, MusicDB.Note, join_through: "artists_notes"
```

```
# lib/music_db/album.ex
many_to_many :notes, MusicDB.Note, join_through: "albums_notes"
```

```
# lib/music_db/track.ex
many_to_many :notes, MusicDB.Note, join_through: "tracks_notes"
```

many_to_many works a little differently than has_many and specifically, we can't use build_assoc to create new associated records. To achieve the same results we've seen in previous examples, we'd have to write the code differently:

```
priv/examples/polymorphism_02.exs
album = Repo.get_by(Album, title: "Kind Of Blue")
note = Repo.insert!(%Note{note: "Love this album!", author: "darin"})
album
|> Repo.preload(:notes)
|> Ecto.Changeset.change()
|> Ecto.Changeset.put_assoc(:notes, [note])
|> Repo.update!
album = Repo.preload(album, :notes)
album.notes
```

Advantages: This works around some of the disadvantages of the first two approaches. We get the benefit of having the association defined in separate tables, but we only need one notes table so we don't have to worry about duplicating our column definitions across several different tables.

Disadvantages: many_to_many is a misnomer in this context. A single note can't (or at least shouldn't) be associated with more than record, but using many_to_many means that would be possible. We'd have to take care to make sure our code doesn't accidentally associate a single note with more than one record. We also can't work with the association in the most intuitive way, due to the differences between has_many and many_to_many.

Wrapping Up

While Ecto doesn't provide direct support for polymorphic associations as some other frameworks do, it's still possible to create these associations, thanks to the flexibility that Ecto's tools provide.

In most cases, we recommend using approach #1 (multiple foreign keys) as it's the most straightforward approach in most respects. However, if the number of foreign keys grows so large as to become cumbersome, you should definitely consider one of the other two approaches. Which of those two you use is largely a matter of personal preference. They will both work well—it's largely just a matter of which feels easier to you.

Ecto's documentation for belongs_to[1] has a section on polymorphic associations and touches on the approaches discussed here. Be sure to check there if you need a refresher on any of these techniques.

---

1. https://hexdocs.pm/ecto/Ecto.Schema.html#belongs_to/3

## CHAPTER 15

Optimizing IEx for Ecto

A perk of working with Elixir is IEx, Elixir's interactive console. With IEx you can peer into a running system to see what's going, or dash out lines of code you'd like to try. For projects using Ecto, IEx provides an alternative to your database console when you want to look up or change parts of your data. Instead of writing raw SQL, you can use Ecto, as done many times in this book.

An often-overlooked benefit of IEx is that it's customizable. When it first launches, it looks for a file called .iex.exs in the current working directory, and then, if it didn't find it, in the user's home directory. If it finds the file, it evaluates it within the same environment as your console session. This means that you can use .iex.exs to set up any import, aliases, or even variables or functions that you frequently use. By adding just a few items to this file, you can streamline your IEx sessions, and save yourself a lot of keystrokes.

In this chapter, we'll offer some suggestions to help you get the most out of using IEx with your Ecto projects.

Adding Imports and Aliases

One of the most useful things you can do is add aliases for the modules you work with often. You'll most likely want to start with Repo and most (if not all) of your schema modules. For the MusicDB app, you might do the following:

priv/examples/optimizing_iex.exs
```
alias MusicDB.{
  Repo,
  Artist,
  Album,
  Track,
  Genre,
  Log
}
```

This one addition means that instead of typing this:

```
album = MusicDB.Repo.get(MusicDB.Album, 1) |> MusicDB.Repo.preload(:tracks)
```

You can type this:

```
album = Repo.get(Album, 1) |> Repo.preload(:tracks)
```

Those saved keystrokes start to add up after a while.

Next, you should import the Ecto.Query module. IEx is a great place to try out queries you're working on, so you'll want to have Query available:

```
import_if_available Ecto.Query
```

We're using import_if_available rather than import so we won't get an error if these modules aren't available. This is less important for an .iex.exs file that's included with a project, as you usually know which dependencies you're using, but if you're using a global .iex.exs this will avoid some headaches.

If you favor the keyword syntax over the macro syntax for your queries (as we have throughout this book), you can be more strategic and limit the import to just the from function, as that's likely to be the only one you'll use:

```
import_if_available Ecto.Query, only: [from: 2]
```

But if you prefer the macro syntax, you'll need to import the whole module.

Lastly, if you think you will want to make changes to your data in IEx, then you will also want to import the Ecto.Changeset module. This will give you the all-important change and cast functions, as well as validations and other utilities:

```
import_if_available Ecto.Changeset
```

Even after including this import, you might find that making changes in IEx is clumsy. You have to load the schema, create a changeset, then hand the changeset to Repo.update. This isn't so bad in the context of your application code, but if you're just trying to make a quick change in the console, it can feel a little verbose. Fortunately, you can use .iex.exs to provide some shortcuts for things like this. We'll explore how to do that next.

Adding Helper Functions

Adding imports and aliases is a good start, but remember that .iex.exs is just a regular Elixir file, so you can define modules and functions as well. Consider the example we were just discussing: making a change to a record in the database. Normally, this process requires a few steps, but you can create a helper function that will handle most of the boilerplate for you.

We usually like to put our IEx helper functions into a single module. And, to help promote the laziness we're trying to achieve, we like to give the module a very short name so it's easy to type. We tend to use like names H or EH for "helper" or "Ecto helper", respectively. Normally, these would be poor choices for module names, as they're not descriptive enough for someone reading our code to understand what they do. But we're creating a module that will only be used within IEx, so we can optimize for easy typing over readability.

Now let's add our new helper function for making changes.

```
priv/examples/optimizing_iex.exs
defmodule H do

  def update(schema, changes) do
    schema
    |> Ecto.Changeset.change(changes)
    |> Repo.update
  end

end
```

This takes any schema struct, then one or more keyword pairs with the values that we want to change. Let's try it out. Exit out of IEx and start it again (with the usual iex -S mix) then try the following:

```
artist = Repo.get_by(Artist, name: "Miles Davis")
H.update(artist, name: "Miles Dewey Davis III",
  birth_date: ~D[1926-05-26])
#=> {:ok,
#=> %MusicDB.Artist{
#=>   __meta__: #Ecto.Schema.Metadata<:loaded, "artists">,
#=>   albums: #Ecto.Association.NotLoaded<association :albums is not loaded>,
#=>   birth_date: ~D[1926-05-26],
#=>   ...
#=>   name: "Miles Dewey Davis III",
#=>   ...
#=> }}
```

That worked. We were able to automate most of the steps of updating a record, and turn them into a one-line function call.

Note that while this approach is fine for our console sessions, this is not something you'd want to have in your application code. We're changing data without any validations or constraint checks, so it would be easy to introduce bad data. That's fine for a development database on your local system that you can easily reconstruct, but for production, you want to be more careful.

Let's try another helper. We might find ourselves frequently looking up albums and their tracks. Let's add a function that will load an album and preload the tracks in a single call:

```
defmodule H do
  #...

  def load_album(id) do
    Repo.get(Album, id) |> Repo.preload(:tracks)
  end
end
```

We might not always know what the album ID is, so let's use pattern matching to define another version of load_album that can accept the album title:

```
defmodule H do
  #...

  def load_album(title) when is_binary(title) do
    Repo.get_by(Album, title: title) |> Repo.preload(:tracks)
  end

  def load_album(id) do
    Repo.get(Album, id) |> Repo.preload(:tracks)
  end
end
```

Normally we might consider adding another definition to catch cases where we pass in something other than an id or a title, but we don't really need to. If we pass in a value that our functions can't handle, we would just get a crash in IEx, and we can live with that.

Wrapping Up

As useful as IEx is on its own, you can make it even more useful by customizing it for your app. If you find that working in IEx feels tedious because you're having to type out full module names, or if you find yourself typing tasks over and over again, it's worth taking a few moments to tweak your .iex.exs file and add it to source control for your project. Your teammates (and future you) will thank you.

IEx has a lot of other powerful features worth exploring. If you'd like to learn more, check out the documentation.[1]

---

1. https://hexdocs.pm/iex/IEx.html

## CHAPTER 16

Using Schemas Without Tables

Some database libraries automatically map database tables to the data structures you use in your application code.

Ecto is not one of them.

Instead, we create our schema structs manually by specifying each of the fields and their types.

At first blush, this can feel like unnecessary work that the framework could be doing for us. But it's actually doing us a service. It allows us to consider the data structures we use in code separately from how that data is stored. This means that we can design our code to be as flexible and expressive as possible, without having to adhere to the rules imposed by relational databases.

In this chapter, we'll start breaking away from developing schemas that exactly match database tables. We'll look at why this can be advantage, and then explore a use case where this separation helps improve the end user experience.

Downsides to Locking Schemas to Tables

When setting up schemas for the first time, it's natural to add fields that exactly match your database tables. But this can have some unintended side effects down the line.

As we've seen, schemas become the backbone of our changesets. And changesets are what we to use parse user-submitted data and convey error messages about that data to the user.

For example, the phoenix_ecto package implements behaviors for the Phoenix web framework such that changesets can be used as the backing data structure for Phoenix forms. To take advantage of the conveniences provided by the Phoenix.Form module, your web forms need to match your changeset structure (and therefore the underlying schema) as much as possible.

Thus, without really intending to, you've turned your database tables into the blueprint for your user interface.

Sometimes this is fine, but tables in relational databases don't always make for user-friendly forms. Tables are bound by a strict set of rules to maximize their efficiency, and that's a completely different concern than how to present a set of fields to an end user in the friendliest manner possible.

Ecto gives us the flexibility to break out of this pattern. Schemas allow us to create data structures that work independently from the database, without losing the conveniences that packages like phoenix_ecto provide.

With Ecto, we can make a distinction between how we collect data, and how we store data.

Breaking Up the Artist Schema

To see how we can make our schemas more flexible, let's consider our artists table. In the most abstract sense, an artist is an entity that produces albums. The simplest representation could be something like this:

- name
- birth_date
- death_date

This looks great for a database table but it would make for a poor UI. If we consider real-world data, we realize that different types of artists exist: bands (The Beatles, Imagine Dragons, King Crimson), and individuals (Imogen Heap, Bob Dylan, Ariana Grande).

For individuals, we'd probably want at least three name fields (we need to handle Sia as well as John Cougar Mellencamp), but bands need just one. The date fields we have here make sense for individuals, but it doesn't feel right to prompt the user for a band's "birth date" and "death date."

That can be remedied by changing the label on the form (we could use something like "start date" rather than "birth date"), but that just masks a deeper problem: bands don't usually have a precise starting date. We more often think in terms of "years active" than start or end date.

From a user's perspective, the two types of artists have different data models that might look something like this:

Solo Artist:

- name1
- name2
- name3
- date_born
- date_died

Band:

- name
- year_started
- year_ended

But even though these two models look different, it wouldn't make sense to have separate tables in the database. The conventions around naming and date nomenclature are a user-facing concern, not a data modeling concern. These two models both have the same relationship to albums and it would be clumsy to try to manage those relationships separately.

So we have a conundrum: we want to be able to use schemas and changesets because of the tools they provide for validation, error reporting, etc. But the data structures we want to present to the user don't map neatly to the database.

Fortunately, Ecto provides a solution: we can create schemas that aren't backed by database tables.

Creating Table-less Schemas

To solve our problem, we'll create two new table-less schemas: one for SoloArtist and another for Band. We'll use these schemas to collect user input, and then translate them into Artist records when it's time to store them.

First, let's set up our new schemas:

```
lib/music_db/solo_artist.ex
defmodule MusicDB.SoloArtist do
  use Ecto.Schema
  import Ecto.Changeset

  embedded_schema do
    field :name1, :string
    field :name2, :string
    field :name3, :string
    field :birth_date, :date
    field :death_date, :date
  end
end
```

```
lib/music_db/band.ex
defmodule MusicDB.Band do
  import Ecto.Changeset
  use Ecto.Schema

  embedded_schema do
    field :name, :string
    field :year_started, :integer
    field :year_ended, :integer
  end
end
```

For the most part, these look quite a lot like the schemas we've been using throughout the book, but we've used embedded_schema rather than schema to declare them. We introduced embedded_schema in Chapter 13, Working with Embedded Schemas, on page 171 as a way to create a schema for JSON data that's stored in a single column. But we can also use it anytime we want to create a schema that isn't directly associated with a database table.

Next, we'll write a changeset function for each schema. We'll use these functions to validate the incoming data and make sure they'll translate correctly into an %Artist{} struct:

```
lib/music_db/solo_artist.ex
def changeset(solo_artist, params) do
  solo_artist
  |> cast(params, [:name1, :name2, :name3, :birth_date, :death_date])
  |> validate_required([:name1, :birth_date])
  # custom validation
  |> validate_date_order(:birth_date, :death_date)
end
```

```
lib/music_db/band.ex
def changeset(band, params) do
  band
  |> cast(params, [:name, :year_started, :year_ended])
  |> validate_required([:name, :year_started])
  # custom validation
  |> validate_year_order(:year_started, :year_ended)
end
```

Each of these functions includes a custom validation that we haven't shown here. validate_date_order will ensure that date_born is earlier than date_died. Similarly in band.ex, validate_year_order will make sure that year_started is less than year_ended.

We'll use these schemas and changesets to present forms to the user. We'll validate the submitted data, and present any errors to the user just as we would with the database-backed schemas we've used before.

Once we've verified that the data is correct, we'll change gears and convert the captured data into Artist records that we can store in the database.

Saving the Table-less Structs

To save the data from these schemas into the artists table, we have a couple of options. One way would be to add extra changeset functions to our Artist schema that take a Band or SoloArtist struct as input:

```
lib/music_db/artist.ex
def changeset(%MusicDB.Band{} = band) do
  {:ok, birth_date} = Date.new(band.year_started, 1, 1)
  {:ok, death_date} = Date.new(band.year_ended, 12, 31)

  changeset(%Artist{
    name: band.name,
    birth_date: birth_date,
    death_date: death_date
  }, %{})
end

def changeset(%MusicDB.SoloArtist{} = solo_artist) do
  name =
    "#{solo_artist.name1} #{solo_artist.name2} #{solo_artist.name3}"
    |> String.trim()

  changeset(%Artist{
    name: name,
    birth_date: solo_artist.birth_date,
    death_date: solo_artist.death_date
  }, %{})
end
```

With this approach, we would validate our Band or SoloArtist changeset and use apply_changes (which we talked about in Chapter 12, Optimizing Your Application Design, on page 161) to get the underlying schema struct with the changes added to it. We could then pass that directly to our new Artist.changeset function:

```
priv/examples/schemas_without_tables.exs
params = %{name: "580 West", year_started: 1991, year_ended: 1995}
band_changeset = Band.changeset(%Band{}, params)
if band_changeset.valid? do
  band_changeset
  |> apply_changes()
  |> Artist.changeset()
  |> Repo.insert!()
else
  # handle validation error
end
```

The Artist changeset would provide another round of validation, which, if we've written our Band and SoloArtist validations correctly, should always complete successfully.

Another approach would be to bypass the Artist struct and create maps or keyword lists that we could pass directly to Repo.insert_all. We could add to_artist functions to Band and SoloArtist to perform the conversion:

```
lib/music_db/band.ex
def to_artist(band) do
  {:ok, birth_date} = Date.new(band.year_started, 1, 1)
  {:ok, death_date} = Date.new(band.year_ended, 12, 31)
  %{name: band.name, birth_date: birth_date, death_date: death_date}
end
```

```
lib/music_db/solo_artist.ex
def to_artist(solo_artist) do
  name =
    "#{solo_artist.name1} #{solo_artist.name2} #{solo_artist.name3}"
    |> String.trim()

  %{name: name, birth_date: solo_artist.birth_date,
    death_date: solo_artist.death_date}
end
```

These two functions generate maps containing names and values of the fields we want to insert into the artists table. We would then take the output of these functions and pass them directly to Repo.insert_all:

```
priv/examples/schemas_without_tables.exs
params = %{name: "580 West", year_started: 1991, year_ended: 1995}
band =
  %Band{}
  |> Band.changeset(params)
  |> apply_changes()

Repo.insert_all("artists", [Band.to_artist(band)])

params = %{name1: "John", name2: "Cougar", name3: "Mellencamp",
  birth_date: ~D[1951-10-07]}
solo_artist =
  %SoloArtist{}
  |> SoloArtist.changeset(params)
  |> apply_changes()

Repo.insert_all("artists", [SoloArtist.to_artist(solo_artist)])
```

Both approaches are valid, and have their pros and cons. With the schema approach, you can continue working with changesets, which can be easier when you need to introspect errors. With insert_all, you have a simpler implementation that doesn't involve layers of schemas. You might experiment and see which option works better for your app.

Wrapping Up

Ecto's schemas require a little manual setup when mapping them to database tables. But in exchange for that effort, you get data structures that are flexible and able to work with the specific needs of your app.

With Ecto, it's possible to break out of the gravitational pull of having your data structures locked to your database tables. You can design your structs around the needs of your application code rather than your database, and still not lose any of the conveniences that changesets provide.

In this chapter, we looked at one use case for table-less schemas, but others exist. In Using Changesets Without Schemas, on page 75, we used the validations from the Changeset module to help validate a search form that we weren't persisting to a database. In that example, we used a map to define the data structure we wanted to validate, but we could have used a table-less schema as well. That might have been a better choice if we wanted to take advantage of some of the other supporting functions that schemas provide. In either case, the idea is the same: Ecto's data manipulation tools are available to you even when you're not working with a relational database.

To see another example of using schemas without tables, see José Valim's blog post "Ecto's insert_all and schemaless queries" on the Plataformatec web site.[1]

---

1. http://blog.plataformatec.com.br/2016/05/ectos-insert_all-and-schemaless-queries

## CHAPTER 17

Tuning for Performance

Ecto gives good performance without the programmer having to think too much about it. The developers of Ecto have put a lot of effort into making it perform well by default, from the higher-level APIs all the way down to the database drivers.

By using macros for its query API, Ecto can compile your queries when your application is compiled. This reduces runtime processing, and allows Ecto to catch query errors early on. Ecto also maintains a cache of prepared queries, greatly reducing the number of times the query has to be prepared and planned by Ecto and the database.

And of course, Ecto sits on top of the Erlang VM, and harnesses the many features it provides to keep your code stable and performant.

It's not uncommon to hear from developers moving to Elixir and Ecto that they were able to remove their application-level caches because the performance was already good enough out of the box. But sometimes, there is more that needs to be done, and in this chapter, we are going to look at some of the things you can tweak to squeeze out more performance.

Bear in mind that when it comes to performance tuning, every application is different and there's rarely a one-size-fits-all solution. As always, it's important to monitor what's going with your app, and make sure that you're clear on exactly where your performance issues lie. With that information in hand, we'll go over a few of the different options you have to change the performance characteristics of Ecto.

Preparing to Optimize

Before you make any changes to your Elixir code to speed things up, remember that optimizing Ecto begins with optimizing your database. If your tables are missing critical indexes, or you're having to perform excessive numbers of joins due to a suboptimal table setup, there's not much that Ecto can do to help. Database optimization is a much bigger topic than we can cover here, but the documentation for your database is good place to start learning about how to get your data into top shape.

You'll also want to make sure that you know exactly where your application is slow. You might think you have a good idea, but unless you've looked at some metrics, you won't know for certain. Ecto's built-in adapters use the Telemetry library to deliver metrics, and we recommend that you look at the "Telemetry Events" section of the Ecto.Repo documentation[1] to learn how to use it to best advantage. Comparing metrics before and after you make changes is the best way to determine that you're moving in the right direction.

Optimizing Queries

One way to optimize your application is to change how it queries for data. As a first step, we have two factors we can consider: bandwidth and latency.

If we optimize for bandwidth, we reduce the amount of data sent from the database to the application. This clears up network congestion, and gives our app less to decode from the database's wire format to Elixir (which also eases the load on the CPU).

If we optimize for latency, we try to reduce the number of queries needed to get the data we want. This can be critical in cloud environments where the round-trip time to the database can be several milliseconds longer than when you have the application and database physically close together. A few milliseconds might not sound like a lot but they can quickly add up. And it's not unusual for applications to do tens of queries for a single web request when working with more complex database structures and many associations.

As mentioned earlier, Ecto already does some work to avoid extra database round-trips, but app developers can apply some techniques to shift the balance between bandwidth and latency. These can help you tune Ecto so that its behavior is best suited for the needs of your application.

To illustrate to these techniques, let's take a look at how we load associations.

---

1. https://hexdocs.pm/ecto/Ecto.Repo.html

Query joins are a common way of loading associated records:

```
from a in Album,
  join: t in assoc(a, :tracks),
  join: ar in assoc(a, :artist),
  preload: [tracks: t, artist: ar]
```

When we use join statements in conjunction with preload, Ecto will perform a single query against the database to fetch all of the records at once. This optimizes for latency, but requires more data to be sent from the database.

This is because artists, albums, and tracks have a has_many relationship connecting them. On most SQL database wire formats, the join statements in the preceding query would return album and artist records along with each track.

Let's say that our database has five artists, each of whom have two albums of ten tracks each. The query would return all one hundred tracks, and each record in the result set would include the associated artist and album records as well. This means that we'd have twenty copies of each artist record, and ten copies of each album. We reduced latency by fetching the records with one query, but in so doing, we strained our bandwidth with a lot of extra data.

If we want to optimize for bandwidth instead of latency, Ecto provides us a few ways to fetch associations with multiple queries rather than a single query with joins. Let's look at a few examples:

```
# Preload with atoms or keyword
from a in Album, preload: [:tracks]

# Preload with anonymous functions
track_fun = fn album_ids ->
  Repo.all(from(t in Track, where: t.album_id in ^album_ids))
end
Repo.all(from(a in Album, preload: [tracks: ^track_fun]))

# Using Repo.preload
albums = Repo.all(Album)
Repo.preload(albums, [:tracks])
```

When using preload without joins, Ecto fetches the associated records with separate queries. This eliminates the duplicate data problem we saw earlier, but adds extra round-trips to the database.

Which approach you should take depends on where your bottleneck lies. It's easy to think that it would be better to have fewer queries, but if your slow performance is due to bandwidth limitations, switching to preload in combination with join could actually make your problem worse.

Another possibility to consider when working with associations is to switch to embedded schemas. You can read more about this option, along with a discussion of the performance trade-offs, in Chapter 13, Working with Embedded Schemas, on page 171.

Finally, keep in mind that with any of these options, you can reduce the amount of data Ecto needs to process by only selecting the columns that you need. If you're using schemas, Ecto's default behavior is to select all the fields you defined. If you have a large schema, this could result in a lot of extra data that you may not be using. But you can always use the select option in your queries to fetch only the columns you want:

```
q = from t in Track, select: [:title, :duration]
Repo.all(q)
```

This will load all of the tracks records in the database, but it will only fetch the title and duration columns of each record. The Track structs in the result set will still have the other fields, but their values will be set to nil.

Executing Bulk Operations

The Repo.update_all and Repo.insert_all operations, first discussed in Chapter 1, Getting Started with Repo, on page 3, allow you to update and insert large groups of records with a single query. Although they're less commonly used than their counterparts update and insert, they can be very efficient for certain use cases.

When using Repo.update, you need to perform one query for each record you want to update. Let's look at how we might reset the number_of_plays counter on our Track records back to 0:

```
tracks = Repo.all(Track)
Enum.each(tracks, fn track ->
  track
  |> Ecto.Changeset.change(%{number_of_plays: 0})
  |> Repo.update!()
end)
```

If our database had 1000 tracks, we'd need to run 1000 queries to reset them all. But by using Repo.update_all we can accomplish the same result with a single query:

```
Repo.update_all(Track, set: [number_of_plays: 0])
```

Apart from :set we can also use :inc to increase a number (you can provide a negative number to decrease the number), :push to add to the end of an array, and :pull to remove from an array. These are atomic operations and they help you avoid having to query for a value, change it, then put it back into the database. But you do give up some control in return. You cannot, for example, guarantee that the arrays you're manipulating contain only unique values. In that case, you would want to use Changeset or Multi to coordinate the operation.

With Repo.insert_all we can perform bulk inserts. Let's say that we're inserting a large number of Artist records. For the following example, we'll assume that artist_records contains a map of raw data that we loaded from a CSV file, or a third-party API:

```
artists =
  Enum.map(artist_records, fn artist ->
    %{name: artist["name"],
      birth_date: artist["birth_date"],
      death_date: artist["death_date"]}
  end)

Repo.insert_all(Artist, artists)
```

This inserts all of the new records into the database with a single query.

One thing to consider with insert_all is the amount of records you're inserting per query. Ecto uses parameterized queries, and most databases have a limit on the number of parameters you can have in a single query. As of this writing, PostgreSQL has a limit of 32,767 and MySQL 65,535. If you're inserting thousands of records, there's a chance that you could run into this limitation.

A good solution is to use Enum.chunk_every/2 to split the records you're inserting into chunks:

```
chunks = Enum.chunk_every(artist_records, 1000)
Enum.each(chunks, fn chunk ->
  artists_chunk =
    Enum.map(chunk, fn artist ->
      %{name: artist["name"],
        birth_date: artist["birth_date"],
        death_date: artist["death_date"]}
    end)
  Repo.insert_all(Artist, artists_chunk)
end)
```

As long as you are inserting less than thirty-three columns per row you can safely chunk by 1000 when using PostgreSQL. Doing this may also reduce the chance of query timeouts when sending a lot of data.

Repo.insert_all has one more trick up its sleeve. You can use the on_conflict option to perform upserts, and let the database decide whether to insert new records or update existing ones. We go over this option in detail in Chapter 11, Inserting and Updating with Upserts, on page 155.

Fetching Large Datasets with Streams

Streams are a core part of Elixir. We use streams for lazy processing, to avoid loading lots of data into memory at once, and even for processing infinite data streams. Many of Elixir's concurrency constructs build on top of streams, such as the Task.async_stream function and the GenStage and Flow packages. It's important to try to utilize concurrency when working with databases because much of the time spent during query execution is waiting for network I/O, during which the CPU is free to do other work.

Throughout much of the book, we've used Repo.all to fetch data from the database. Repo.stream is its stream-based counterpart. It returns a lazy stream that can work with a database as its source.

Like other Elixir streams, it won't start loading data until it is used and traversed, and you can use it in combination with other functions in the Stream module. Repo.stream only fetches rows from the database when they are needed —by default, it fetches in chunks of 500 at a time.

Let's look at an example of using Repo.stream to process a large number of records. Say that we want to dump all of our artists records out to a file on our local filesystem. Here's how we might use streams to accomplish this (assume for the moment that save_artist_record is a function that writes the record to a file):

```
stream =
  Artist
  |> Repo.stream()
  |> Task.async_stream(fn artist ->
    save_artist_record(artist)
  end)
Repo.transaction(fn ->
  Stream.run(stream)
end)
```

Note the use of Repo.transaction around the Stream.run call. We say that a stream is "realized" when we start traversing it using any of the Enum functions or Stream.run. Any stream we create with Repo.stream must be realized inside a transaction. For long-running streams, you may need to increase the transaction timeout by passing the :timeout option to Repo.transaction. The default timeout is 15 seconds, but you can use this option to set the timeout to any value you like, including :infinity.

While a transaction is active, it's holding a database connection from the pool, so you need to be careful not to tie up all of your connections with long-running transactions. If this becomes a problem, you might consider building up your own stream using Elixir's Stream.resource function.

The following example uses this approach to run multiple queries over a dataset using limit and offset:

```
query = from(Artist, order_by: [:id])
chunk_size = 500
offset = 0

stream =
  Stream.resource(
    fn -> 0 end,
    fn
      :stop -> {:halt, :stop}
      offset ->
        rows =
          Repo.all(from(query, limit: ^chunk_size, offset: ^offset))
        if Enum.count(rows) < chunk_size do
          {rows, :stop}
        else
          {rows, offset + chunk_size}
        end
    end,
    fn _ -> :ok end
  )
```

This stream will perform a new query for each set of 500 rows by limiting each result to 500 rows and increasing the offset by 500 for each query.

The benefit is that we can run this query outside of a transaction, so we are not limited to transaction timeouts and we are not locking up a connection while we are traversing the stream. The downside is that because we are running outside of a transaction, the result may be inconsistent. If another process adds or removes records while we're traversing the stream, we may miss some records, or see duplicates of others. This may be acceptable in some cases; if not, you may be able to work around this by running the stream more than once, and marking processed rows so that they can be skipped on the next run.

Wrapping Up

As we mentioned at the beginning of this chapter, optimizing for performance is an app-specific process. What works beautifully on one app could be catastrophic on another. It all depends on what the requirements and constraints are.

Ecto was designed with performance in mind, and this chapter outlined some techniques you can use to make it go even faster. But before you try any or all of these, it's important to use metrics to determine exactly what is and isn't going slowly in your app. Once you've identified where the problem is, you can decide if you need to change something at the database level, or change the way you're using Ecto to get the performance you need.

Bibliography

[Tho18]   Dave Thomas. *Programming Elixir ≥ 1.6*. The Pragmatic Bookshelf, Raleigh, NC, 2018.

[TV18]   Chris McCord, Bruce Tate and José Valim. *Programming Phoenix ≥ 1.4*. The Pragmatic Bookshelf, Raleigh, NC, 2018.

Index

Thank you!

How did you enjoy this book? Please let us know. Take a moment and email us at support@pragprog.com with your feedback. Tell us your story and you could win free ebooks. Please use the subject line "Book Feedback."

Ready for your next great Pragmatic Bookshelf book? Come on over to https://pragprog.com and use the coupon code BUYANOTHER2019 to save 30% on your next ebook.

Void where prohibited, restricted, or otherwise unwelcome. Do not use ebooks near water. If rash persists, see a doctor. Doesn't apply to *The Pragmatic Programmer* ebook because it's older than the Pragmatic Bookshelf itself. Side effects may include increased knowledge and skill, increased marketability, and deep satisfaction. Increase dosage regularly.

And thank you for your continued support,

Andy Hunt, Publisher

Craft GraphQL APIs in Elixir with Absinthe

Your domain is rich and interconnected, and your API should be too. Upgrade your web API to GraphQL, leveraging its flexible queries to empower your users, and its declarative structure to simplify your code. Absinthe is the GraphQL toolkit for Elixir, a functional programming language designed to enable massive concurrency atop robust application architectures. Written by the creators of Absinthe, this book will help you take full advantage of these two groundbreaking technologies. Build your own flexible, high-performance APIs using step-by-step guidance and expert advice you won't find anywhere else.

Bruce Williams and Ben Wilson
(302 pages) ISBN: 9781680502558. $47.95
https://pragprog.com/book/wwgraphql

Property-Based Testing with PropEr, Erlang, and Elixir

Property-based testing helps you create better, more solid tests with little code. By using the PropEr framework in both Erlang and Elixir, this book teaches you how to automatically generate test cases, test stateful programs, and change how you design your software for more principled and reliable approaches. You will be able to better explore the problem space, validate the assumptions you make when coming up with program behavior, and expose unexpected weaknesses in your design. PropEr will even show you how to reproduce the bugs it found. With this book, you will be writing efficient property-based tests in no time.

Fred Hebert
(374 pages) ISBN: 9781680506211. $45.95
https://pragprog.com/book/fhproper

Programming Elixir 1.6

This book is *the* introduction to Elixir for experienced programmers, completely updated for Elixir 1.6 and beyond. Explore functional programming without the academic overtones (tell me about monads just one more time). Create concurrent applications, but get them right without all the locking and consistency headaches. Meet Elixir, a modern, functional, concurrent language built on the rock-solid Erlang VM. Elixir's pragmatic syntax and built-in support for metaprogramming will make you productive and keep you interested for the long haul. Maybe the time is right for the Next Big Thing. Maybe it's Elixir.

Dave Thomas
(410 pages) ISBN: 9781680502992. $47.95
https://pragprog.com/book/elixir16

Programming Phoenix 1.4

Don't accept the compromise between fast and beautiful: you can have it all. Phoenix creator Chris McCord, Elixir creator José Valim, and award-winning author Bruce Tate walk you through building an application that's fast and reliable. At every step, you'll learn from the Phoenix creators not just what to do, but why. Packed with insider insights and completely updated for Phoenix 1.4, this definitive guide will be your constant companion in your journey from Phoenix novice to expert, as you build the next generation of web applications.

Chris McCord, Bruce Tate and José Valim
(325 pages) ISBN: 9781680502268. $45.95
https://pragprog.com/book/phoenix14

Functional Web Development with Elixir, OTP, and Phoenix

Elixir and Phoenix are generating tremendous excitement as an unbeatable platform for building modern web applications. For decades OTP has helped developers create incredibly robust, scalable applications with unparalleled uptime. Make the most of them as you build a stateful web app with Elixir, OTP, and Phoenix. Model domain entities without an ORM or a database. Manage server state and keep your code clean with OTP Behaviours. Layer on a Phoenix web interface without coupling it to the business logic. Open doors to powerful new techniques that will get you thinking about web development in fundamentally new ways.

Lance Halvorsen
(218 pages) ISBN: 9781680502435. $45.95
https://pragprog.com/book/lhelph

Adopting Elixir

Adoption is more than programming. Elixir is an exciting new language, but to successfully get your application from start to finish, you're going to need to know more than just the language. You need the case studies and strategies in this book. Learn the best practices for the whole life of your application, from design and team-building, to managing stakeholders, to deployment and monitoring. Go beyond the syntax and the tools to learn the techniques you need to develop your Elixir application from concept to production.

Ben Marx, José Valim, Bruce Tate
(242 pages) ISBN: 9781680502527. $42.95
https://pragprog.com/book/tvmelixir

Software Design X-Rays

Are you working on a codebase where cost overruns, death marches, and heroic fights with legacy code monsters are the norm? Battle these adversaries with novel ways to identify and prioritize technical debt, based on behavioral data from how developers work with code. And that's just for starters. Because good code involves social design, as well as technical design, you can find surprising dependencies between people and code to resolve coordination bottlenecks among teams. Best of all, the techniques build on behavioral data that you already have: your version-control system. Join the fight for better code!

Adam Tornhill
(274 pages) ISBN: 9781680502725. $45.95
https://pragprog.com/book/atevol

Release It! Second Edition

A single dramatic software failure can cost a company millions of dollars—but can be avoided with simple changes to design and architecture. This new edition of the best-selling industry standard shows you how to create systems that run longer, with fewer failures, and recover better when bad things happen. New coverage includes DevOps, microservices, and cloud-native architecture. Stability antipatterns have grown to include systemic problems in large-scale systems. This is a must-have pragmatic guide to engineering for production systems.

Michael Nygard
(376 pages) ISBN: 9781680502398. $47.95
https://pragprog.com/book/mnee2

The Pragmatic Bookshelf

The Pragmatic Bookshelf features books written by developers for developers. The titles continue the well-known Pragmatic Programmer style and continue to garner awards and rave reviews. As development gets more and more difficult, the Pragmatic Programmers will be there with more titles and products to help you stay on top of your game.

Visit Us Online

This Book's Home Page
https://pragprog.com/book/wmecto
Source code from this book, errata, and other resources. Come give us feedback, too!

Keep Up to Date
https://pragprog.com
Join our announcement mailing list (low volume) or follow us on twitter @pragprog for new titles, sales, coupons, hot tips, and more.

New and Noteworthy
https://pragprog.com/news
Check out the latest pragmatic developments, new titles and other offerings.

Save on the eBook

Save on the eBook versions of this title. Owning the paper version of this book entitles you to purchase the electronic versions at a terrific discount.

PDFs are great for carrying around on your laptop—they are hyperlinked, have color, and are fully searchable. Most titles are also available for the iPhone and iPod touch, Amazon Kindle, and other popular e-book readers.

Buy now at *https://pragprog.com/coupon*

Contact Us

Online Orders:	*https://pragprog.com/catalog*
Customer Service:	*support@pragprog.com*
International Rights:	*translations@pragprog.com*
Academic Use:	*academic@pragprog.com*
Write for Us:	*http://write-for-us.pragprog.com*
Or Call:	+1 800-699-7764